A–Z of Prayer

Building strong foundations for daily conversations with God

Matthew Porter

First published 2019 by Authentic Media Limited,
PO Box 6326, Bletchley, Milton Keynes, MK1 9GG.
authenticmedia.co.uk

British Library Cataloguing in Publication Data
A catalogue record for this book is available from the British Library.
ISBN: 978-1-78893-062-8
978-1-78893-063-5 (e-book)

Cover design by Luke Porter
Printed and bound by CPI Group (UK) Ltd., Croydon, CR0 4YY

Contents

Foreword   v
Preface   vii

Introduction   1
A is for Adoration   5
B is for Belief   13
C is for Confession   21
D is for Devotion   27
E is for Extemporary   35
F is for Fasting   43
G is for Gratitude   51
H is for Honesty   57
I is for Intercession   65
J is for Joyful   73
K is for Kenosis   79
L is for Liturgy   87
M is for Morning   93
N is for Night   101
O is for Opportunity   109
P is for Prophetic   117
Q is for Quiet   125

Contents

R is for Relentless 133

S is for Sad 141

T is for Tongues 149

U is for Unanswered 157

V is for Vision 165

W is for Warfare 173

X is for eXamen 181

Y is for Yearning 187

Z is for Zero 195

Afterword 203

Notes 205

Index 228

Foreword

I was thrilled when Matthew told me he was writing a book on prayer. His previous book *A–Z of Discipleship* has been so helpful to lots of people; I knew this would be a winner too.

I have been on a journey of prayer since I started following Jesus in 1975 at the tender age of 8. I have given my life more fully to prayer in the last twelve years, pioneering a house of prayer with my wife and team in the Midlands.

I have prayed much and have observed many people praying. People say that prayer is more 'caught' than 'taught'. I would say 'yes' and 'no' to that. Yes certainly, you are stimulated to pray more by life, faith, other believers and God's work in your life, than by attending a course or seminar. That is because prayer is part of a living, breathing, active, constantly changing relationship with God as you navigate life. You can't bottle it up in formulas or package it up in simple 'three step' principles.

Yet, as the history of the Christian faith has shown, one *can* be taught and helped to pray. Just as a child learns language by interaction, guidance, correction and much encouragement by the adults and older children in their life, so a Christian believer does need some training and encouragement to grow in prayer. Jesus' disciples saw his vibrant prayer life with Father God and then asked him to teach them to pray. A life of prayer is at the same time a maturing in language, a deepening relationship, a house of treasures to explore, and a key to live a life of faith.

Matthew's book *A–Z of Prayer* is a book that really teaches you to pray. To pray more, to pray better, to pray as if your life depends on it. It is also a book full of testimonies; it is a 'how to' manual and it is a spiritual journey.

For those who are looking for spiritual guidance on the most important topic of prayer, they will find it in shedloads in this book. For people who think Christian prayer is a bit of a mystery, this will demystify jargon and make prayer a life-giving pathway to communicating with God. For believers who have become dry in their prayer lives, this will be a refreshing read and way back into a revitalized walk with God. Even for mature Christians, there will be some surprises in this book, and maybe ways of praying that will be new to them.

Matthew too prays much; his inner spiritual life is now offering him opportunities to share his learning, the fruit of his ministry and his passion for God. As his brother, I am delighted to champion this book. I will be passing it on to my friends and fellow prayer-ers and would encourage you to read it and let your prayer life be refreshed or turned upside down!

William Porter, Team Leader, Beacon House of Prayer, Stoke-on-Trent, UK

Preface

I've written this short book on prayer because it's important.[1] It really is imperative to pray! It's through prayer that we get to know God. It's through prayer that we mature as disciples of Jesus Christ. And it's through prayer that the world is transformed.

I've written this short book on prayer because it's needed. There are many books on Christian prayer – in fact, thousands – but few that are simple and could be given to someone who knows little or nothing about following Jesus or feels like they're a novice at prayer.[2] This book is for people just like that.

I've written this short book on prayer because it's timely. In the Western Church, and particularly in the UK where I live, the Lord is calling his church to return to its foundations and do a few things well – one of which is prayer.[3]

I hope this book is useful to many and a helpful addition to the A–Z series that began with my *A–Z of Discipleship*, published in 2017, which aimed at building strong foundations for a life of following Jesus. This book aims to do something similar, but applied to prayer, which is building strong foundations for daily conversations with God.

With grateful thanks to Sophie Dearden, James Fletcher, Warren Furman, Luke Porter, Sam Porter, William Porter, Ruth

Preface

Somerville and Barry Smith for your helpful comments on early drafts of this manuscript.

Matthew Porter
St Michael le Belfrey, York

This book is dedicated to those who've taught me to pray.

To my two grandfathers – Luther Porter and Wilfred Brown. As a boy I loved to hear them pray.

To my father – Richard Porter. Who modelled prayer to me more than any other person.

To my mother – Christine Porter. Your prayerfulness continues to be an inspiration.

To my brother – William Porter. Thank you for all you've faithfully pioneered.

To my wife – Sam Porter. I love the way you pray from the heart with simplicity and compassion.

To my friend – James Fletcher. Thank you for being devoted to prayer, and for starting such a good work in St Cuthbert's House of Prayer in York.

Introduction

This *A–Z of Prayer* is a short, simple, no-nonsense guide to prayer.

Prayer is communication with God – what Clement, a second-century church leader, called 'a conversation with God.'[1] It's talking to God and with God. But it's also listening and letting him speak back to us. That can only happen out of relationship.

Some people don't realize that they're made for relationship with God, but we are. We all are. God made us to know us and for us to know him. If we don't live in relationship with God then we're not fully alive. Not fully human. Not fully the person we were designed to be. If that's you – if you're not yet living life in relationship with God – then you can make a start right now and begin the great adventure of following Jesus. The best way to do that is to start praying and start reading the Bible (probably beginning with one of the four Gospel accounts of Jesus – e.g. Mark). As you do those two things, you will find yourself opening up to the presence of God and beginning to hear his voice, to which you can respond with further prayer.

The Bible is God's inspired word and the handbook for discipleship for the follower of Jesus. It should inform all our thinking, living and praying, which is why it's good to pray with an open Bible. In fact, as we'll discover in this A–Z, it's good to use the Bible as our prayerbook, praying biblical themes and often turning Scripture to prayer.

If you don't know where to start with prayer, just start! Many begin with something like, 'God, if you're there, please show yourself to me.' You might want to go further and start to tell him what's on your mind and heart. Be open. Be honest. Be you.

When you pray, be yourself. Talk to God like you would talk with a friend. Have daily conversations with him. He knows you well – in fact, better than you know yourself – so there's no need to put on a mask or pretend. He sees our hearts and loves us with a passion, for he is our good Father who has made us. He has revealed himself to us most perfectly in Jesus Christ, and it's this Jesus who calls us to follow him. He also gives us his Spirit to be with us, to encourage us and empower us – especially to pray.

Praying is sometimes the easiest and most natural thing to do. We just talk to God because we can. Because Jesus has opened the gate to heaven and there is nothing stopping us! But there are other times when prayer is difficult. It feels like hard work. You may not want to pray or you might feel like your prayers are hitting a brick wall. Whether it's easy or whether it's difficult, you need to keep praying. Every day. That's because breakthrough is often just the other side of your next passionate prayer. But many never see it as they give up too easily. Don't do that. Pray. And keep praying.[2] For the benefits will be immense.

> Breakthrough is often just the other side of your next passionate prayer.

If you want some inspiration to pray, be encouraged that both Jesus and the Holy Spirit are praying and talking with the Father (what the Bible calls 'interceding' – see **I is for Intercession**) on your behalf. The Bible tells us just this – that 'Christ Jesus who died . . . is at the right hand of God and is also interceding for us'[3] and that 'the Spirit helps us in our weakness . . .

And . . . intercedes for God's people in accordance with the will of God'.[4]

This is very good news! It reassures us that our prayers are backed up by God himself. If that's not an encouragement to pray, then I don't know what is!

So the bottom line is that we must pray. You don't need to be a disciple for long to realize this. But how do we pray? How can we do it effectively and confidently? That's what this book is all about – wanting to give some basic information and simple suggestions on prayer that will especially help equip new disciples to become people of prayer.

As this book has twenty-six short chapters, it won't take you very long to read it all in one go. However, if you want to get the most out of it, I'd urge you to read it slowly, taking a chapter each day, giving time to work on the short *Action* and *Prayer* sections at the end of each chapter and writing your reflections down – either in the space provided or in a notebook, or if you're reading on Kindle by using the 'Add Notes' section. First thing in the morning would be best, enabling you to chew over and then put into practice the chapter's theme as you go through your day. Reading the *A–Z of Prayer* in this way will take you just under a month.

My prayer for you as you read this book is that you will find it one of the most impactful months of your life, and that the Holy Spirit will draw close to you, speak to you and bring you lasting transformation.

For further resources related to this book, go to https://azprayer.org.

Matthew Porter can be contacted at matthew.porter@belfrey.org.

A is for Adoration

It's one of the most beautiful sounds in the world. The sound of people simultaneously praying prayers of adoration to God. It often makes the hairs rise on the back of my neck and stirs my heart like nothing else. It's delightful and delicious. Wonderful and warm. Loving and lovely. It's the sound of adoration.

Adoration is telling someone how much you appreciate and love them. Disciples do this in prayer to God. They adore God. In spoken word or in song. In unison or on your own.

When Jesus was asked by his first disciples to teach them to pray, he gave them what we now call *The Lord's Prayer*.[1] The first words of that prayer are words of adoration:

Our Father in heaven, hallowed be your name . . .

That was the very first thing Jesus taught his followers about prayer. That they should start with adoration.[2] That's why this *A–Z of Prayer* starts with **A is for Adoration**.[3]

> Adoration was the very first thing Jesus taught his followers about prayer.

Adoration is basic to who we are and what we do, in response to what God has done for us in Jesus Christ. It's not just what *I'm* called to do, but also what God's people are *corporately* invited to do, for he is 'our' Father. He has made us and loves us. He sent Jesus to bring the kingdom of heaven to earth, to die and rise to forgive us and to give us a brand new start. He fills us with his life-giving Spirit, empowering us to live with fresh identity, authority and love. He has done so much for us and continues to surprise us with his goodness. Such is his love! How else can we respond, except with adoration?

The Bible tells us that we love God because he first loved us.[4] The language of this love is the language of adoration. It's the language of friends. Partners. Lovers. It's saying 'I love you' in all sorts of ways.

If you're reading this and are concerned that this all sounds like sentimental nonsense for the contemporary age, be aware that followers of Jesus have been adoring God for all of church history. St Ambrose of Milan (337–397) prayed that God would give him 'a heart to love and adore you, a heart to delight in you, to follow and enjoy you, for Christ's sake'.[5] Anselm (1033–1109) similarly modelled what it is to pray prayers of adoration, praying 'Lord, because you have made me, I owe you the whole of my love.'[6] In 1744 Francis Wade expressed such a desire by adapting an older Christmas song about the birth of Jesus – a song still much sung today, called 'O Come All Ye Faithful' – which includes the simple but profound words 'O come let us adore him, O come let us adore him, O come let us adore him, Christ the Lord.'

Adoration has always been at the heart of Christian prayer.

When I think of adoration, I think of Bill Johnson, the author and senior pastor of Bethel Church in Redding, California. I was at a conference recently where he was one of the keynote speakers. He had travelled thousands of miles to be at this conference and was tired. At one point in the opening session I looked around in the worship and my gaze rested on him as he stood there, eyes closed, singing to God with hands reaching out, giving his love and devotion to Christ. Neither tiredness, nor age, nor any other circumstances were going to stop him adoring Jesus with a passion. He knows this is the right response to the God who has given his best to and for us. Adoration is the right response to the goodness of God.

For thousands of years God's people have known that 'the Lord is good and his love endures for ever'.[7] The first of the Ten Commandments in the Old Testament is a command to adore only this God.[8] Jesus summarized this by telling disciples to 'Love the Lord your God with all your heart and with all your soul and with all your mind and with all your strength'.[9] Disciples express this love with their lives and with their words. When we use words to tell God how much we value him, we are adoring him.

Adoration is intimate. It's meant to be. Bill Johnson's wife, Beni, who is a person of prayer, summarizes this beautifully by saying that 'when we adore God, we are kissing him'.[10] We are drawing near, in love. We enjoy his presence and he enjoys ours. We can come near because Jesus has opened the gate of heaven. Through Christ's death and resurrection any barriers between us and God have been removed. God is close. And he calls us to draw close in adoration.[11]

> God is close. And he calls us to draw close in adoration.

How do we do this? There are lots of ways. If you're not sure where to start, start with those opening words of *The Lord's Prayer* – 'hallowed be/holy is your name' – and then use them as a springboard to speaking further words of love to God. This is an intimate and deep thing, and if you're not used to doing that with another person, you might not find it easy at first. If that's you, persevere. (Also, learning to adore God will help you and give you confidence in adoring others. I am definitely better at adoring my wife now I have more experience in adoring God – and I think she likes it!) Even if your words run out, do your best to tell God from the heart how much you value him. You can use prayer-words that others have written (see **L is for Liturgy**) or the words of songs can also help. The most important thing is to do it.

Sometimes we come to God with a list of things for prayer. God doesn't mind this. He wants to hear our *please prayers* (see **I is for Intercession**). But if we can, it's good to start with adoration. We've been learning this at our prayer centre in York, St Cuthbert's House of Prayer. By adoring before we intercede we're saying to the Lord, 'You are bigger than anything that I'm about to pray about.' King Solomon did just this when he dedicated to God the very first temple built in Israel, beginning his prayers by praying: 'LORD, the God of Israel, there is no God like you in heaven above or on earth below – you who keep your covenant of love with your servants . . .'[12]

Often when I spend time in adoration I find I'm filled with a profound sense of awe at who God is. As I focus on him, recalling what he's done through Christ in history, and all he's done in my life, I am amazed and I want to revere him. So I give him my love, but often it feels like my words and my songs and the way I express all this with my body just aren't enough. That's why sometimes I stop speaking or singing, and I just rest in his presence, allowing my very being to become an object of worship. Such moments are precious as I experience a deep connection in the Holy Spirit. This can happen anywhere and often feels likes the gap between heaven and earth is very thin – because it is!

In heaven, there is much adoration taking place. We get a glimpse of this in the last book of the Bible – the book of

Revelation. In Revelation we see elders gathered round the throne of God, casting their crowns before him in an act of humility and giving Christ their praise and their love, saying: 'You are worthy, our Lord and God, to receive glory and honour and power . . .'[13] When we adore God like this today, we're bringing heaven to earth.

If you're new to prayer you might be concerned about posture – that is, what you do with your body when you pray. The Bible has much to say on this, encouraging us to use our bodies to express our prayers. That's why many pray with their hands raised or stretched out.[14] In the ancient catacombs of the first churches in places such as Rome, there are paintings on the ceilings of early Christians in worship and prayer, and their hands are raised, so this is a common and ancient practice of the church. Sometimes it's helpful to kneel, as a sign of reverence and humility.[15] Some especially do this when saying sorry to God in confession (see **C is for Confession**). Occasionally people lie flat on their face before God.[16] When prayer and worship turns from adoration to praise (see **G is for Gratitude**) it can be good to clap[17] and dance.[18] When this is done with others it's not only great fun but also deeply powerful, as corporate adoration and praise impacts our surroundings.

But none of this should take away from the simple act of an individual disciple waking each morning and beginning to adore God, and then living a life of adoration. This is not just acknowledging his presence but appreciating him and giving him love. Adoration is basic to prayer and foundational to our relationship with the God who loves us more than we can imagine with a love that is wonderfully profound and deeply personal, in Jesus Christ.

What else can we do, but adore him?

ACTION: Think about why you appreciate God. What is it about him that you love? Then either in a notebook or in the space below, write down some words and phrases that say something of your love for God.

Determine to become more a person of adoration. Someone who adores God. Every day. But also resolve to grow in ways of appreciating people around you, telling them how much you value them. Think of one person and choose what you will do to show them your appreciation today – maybe speak to them in person, or send them a text, or write them a letter.

PRAYER: Begin to put this chapter into practice straight away, by adoring God. Use some of the words and phrases you wrote down to help you. Start with the opening words of *The Lord's Prayer*: 'Our Father in heaven, hallowed by your name'. Begin to call on God – the One who is your loving Father. And not only yours, but 'ours'. Remind yourself that you are joining with billions of people adoring him today. Thank him for his love and his holiness – for his godliness and goodness – and all he is. Allow your prayers to articulate your love. Use your body to express this love. Honour and revere him with your words, and ask for his Spirit to help you live today in a way that reflects this adoration.

Further Reading:

Rolland and Heidi Baker, *Reckless Devotion* (Maidstone: River Publishing, 2014).

B is for Belief

Prayer is not just talking into the dark to a God who might just possibly be there. Whether people realize it or not, when they pray they're actually conversing with the very Creator of the universe who is present, personal and powerful, and who loves to hear our prayers! That's what Jesus modelled to his disciples[1] and it's why he urged them to pray and taught them to pray.[2] So when we pray, God wants us to believe that he's there and that he wants to answer our prayers.[3] In short, we are to pray in faith. Jesus says just this in Mark 11:24: 'Whatever you ask for in prayer, believe that you have received it . . .' That's why **B is for Belief**.

In 2017 a follower of Jesus who lived in a different city, sixty miles from York, was suffering from a bad back and was praying. As he prayed he sensed the Lord say, 'Go to St Michael le Belfrey Church in York and you will be healed.' So the next Sunday evening he came to our church in York and went forward for prayer towards the end of the service.[4] He was paired up with two people and told them his story. As he described how God had spoken to him, Chris, one of the two, felt faith rise up in him. Chris became convinced that God must have sent this man to us because he wanted him healed. So, believing that God wanted to heal him, they prayed with authority, commanding the back to be healed in the name of Jesus. And it was. Right there and then. The man described a heat sensation going through his back, and then tested it out, doing all sorts of stretching and jumping which he couldn't do before. He was overjoyed! As were those who prayed.

On a number of occasions Jesus said 'your faith has healed you'[5] to people who came to him believing that they'd be healed. Clearly he meant that *God* had healed them, but that their *faith* had played an important part in activating God's healing power. That's because while God always hears and receives our prayers, for lasting transformation to take place there needs to be some faith. Some belief. Jesus made this abundantly clear to his disciples, saying that sometimes their prayers were not effective because there was no faith – no belief that God will do what is asked.[6]

Some people make a distinction between faith and belief. While there are occasionally some minor semantic differences in the way we use the word in English, in Greek they are the same, both being possible translations of the same Greek word *pistis*. Bible translators sometimes choose one rather than the other depending on the context, but in essence faith and belief are identical. That's why faith can be defined simply as 'belief that God will'.[7] We need this faith/belief when we pray. It's the active ingredient that gets God's attention[8] and releases the power of the kingdom of God.

We discover from the stories of Jesus that this kind of transformational belief can reside in all sorts of people. Sometimes it's found in the person seeking God's help – which is why Jesus says 'your faith has healed you' to the woman who reached out and touched his robe.[9] On other occasions faith is located with someone else in the situation, such as a friend or family member – which was the case in the story of the sick man who was healed as a result of his friends making a hole in the roof, so they could lower him into the room below where Jesus was![10]

The main thing is that somewhere, someone is praying with some faith.

Sometimes people ask how much faith is needed when we come to God in prayer. Jesus answered this, basically saying *very little*. He said that faith as small as a tiny mustard seed could move a mountain![11] That's why, in my *A–Z of Discipleship,* I say that 'what's most important is not that we have great faith but that we have faith in a great God'.[12]

> What's important is not that we have great faith but that we have faith in a great God.

When I was a young man at university, I read the book *Prayer: Key to Revival* by Paul Y. Cho. I was challenged by the way he prayed and by his simple belief in a great God. He was often very specific in his prayers, both for himself, his family, his church and his nation. He learned to pray *believing prayers*. When I think of a person praying prayers of great faith, I think of Paul Y. Cho. He knew that praying in faith is not about first having to psyche ourselves up so that we really believe something's going to happen. It's about trusting that God is good and loving and powerful. It can help to remind ourselves of his character and his purposes. This often happens as we worship and adore him (see **A is for Adoration**) and particularly as we read Scripture. Having done that we can then ask him what he would like to do. Often when we do this we gain a sense of his desires and that helps us to pray in faith – with real belief.

If you want to be inspired to be a person of faith, praying faith-filled prayers, then you need look no further in the Bible than Hebrews chapter 11. There we find a list of past heroes who prayed in faith and then turned their prayers into action. It's the faith behind their actions that's particularly commended. We're given a summary of their lives, which are described in more detail elsewhere in the Old Testament. As we hear these stories of old, so faith – belief that God will – grows.

Faith is also stirred as we hear testimony of what God is doing amongst us today. We've found at The Belfrey that it's good to share such stories before we pray. Hearing stories of answered prayer often causes people to think, 'if God has done that for them, he can do that for me' and so they respond and pray, or ask for prayer. We see a good example of this in the Bible in the woman who Jesus met at Jacob's well. Through this encounter with Jesus, recorded in John 4, her life was turned around and she became 'a believer'. She told her story to the people of her community, who then went to see Jesus and as a result believed for themselves.[13] This shows us that testimony is not just about giving praise for what God has done. Testimony also has the effect of releasing faith, which means it provides an opportunity for God to work again. We see this many times in the Bible, where in prayer people remind themselves – and God – of what he's done in the past, and then ask him to come in power and do it again.[14]

I've noticed that prayerful communities who regularly share testimony often become places of great faith. A culture is created where there's a deep and genuine conviction that God answers prayer, and probably will once more. Having seen and heard so many stories of changed lives and transformed situations, there's an expectation that the Lord will do it again. Often when I'm in such communities I sense the presence of God and I'm moved to pray, sometimes with fresh faith and vigour.

It's good to be creative when we pray. I keep a journal where I record all sorts of things, including testimonies of answered prayer plus some of my prayers, especially when I've asked for something that feels like a real step of trusting faith. Writing my prayers feels different to speaking my prayers. And it is, with studies showing that speaking and writing use very different parts of our brain.[15]

The imagination is one of the loveliest and most powerful gifts God has given us, and it can be used in many creative ways as we pray. One way is to imagine an outcome of the thing you're praying for, and then ask God for that mental picture to become reality. For example, people often ask me to pray with them for a loved-one who's not yet following Jesus. Sometimes they say that they've been praying for a while and feel like they've got little or no faith that it will happen. So I sometimes ask them to imagine the person doing something they would do when they start following Jesus – like reading the Bible, or joining in worship. Often at that point I notice them smiling as they begin to picture this. It's like a spark of faith begins to arise and it helps them pray again, believing that the Lord wants to draw their loved-one into God's kingdom.

Another way to be creative is to draw or paint our prayers. Using the imagination we can then put on paper our hopes and desires and express the cries of our hearts to God. Sometimes when we do this, it stirs faith. Sometimes it does that in others too. That's why I love looking at the prayers others have drawn or painted. We often hang them on the walls in our House of Prayer. I find they cause faith to rise in me.

But what should we do if we have little or no faith for a situation? Does that mean we shouldn't pray? Not at all! Pray anyway. It's good and OK to ask for more belief.[16] God doesn't mind that. But sometimes it's hard to know if we have faith for a particular situation. So just pray anyway. Pray despite having doubts. Because God loves to hear our prayers, and often surprises us. In fact, while God particularly responds to faith, he also responds to obedience.

> Sometimes it's hard to know if we have faith for a particular situation. So just pray anyway. Pray despite having doubts.

I've found on many occasions I've prayed prayers that seem to have very little faith behind them, and yet God has answered them anyway! I might pray for financial provision for someone. Or for healing. Or for someone's circumstances to change. Maybe I'm tired or it's just a short passing prayer as I'm on the way to something and my prayers are not particularly faith-filled. And yet quite often the Lord answers them. I can think of Barry Smith, who last year joined the small group I'm part of. One evening, as the group was gathering in the kitchen I commented on the nice smell of brewing coffee, and he said that he wouldn't know, having lost his sense of smell and taste a number of years ago. So I pulled in someone else standing nearby and together we prayed a simple prayer, asking the Lord to restore his ability to smell. I'm not sure if they, like me, had much faith that his smell would return. But we prayed anyway. Nothing happened that evening, but when I saw him a few days later he was amazed, telling me that he was starting to enjoy all sorts of smells, and over the coming months his smell *and* taste returned. On reflection, our short simple prayers that night felt more like obedient prayers than faith-filled prayers. How much faith did we have that Barry would be healed? Maybe just about a mustard seed amount! But the Lord did it anyway. I am thankful. And Barry is too!

ACTION: Think of a prayer that you've prayed that God has answered. Write it down in the space below or in your notebook.

Read Psalm 65. It says (in v. 2) that God answers prayer. Some examples of answered prayer are then given (in v. 3, v. 4, and then from v. 5). Take note of these and write them down. Recognise that through Jesus Christ, the Lord has done the same for you, answering your prayers.

As you consider what God has done, let faith – belief that God will – rise up in you. Now think of another situation where you'd love to see transformation. Write the situation down here or in your notebook.

PRAYER: Now begin to pray. Ask the Spirit of God what he would like to do in the situation you've just been considering. Allow your thoughts to be guided in prayer. Now ask.

Ask him to help you to trust him more and more and be increasingly expectant that he will use your prayers, as much as those of others.

End by thanking God for who he is – picking up the description you noted from Psalm 65.

Further Reading:

Pete Greig, *Dirty Glory* (London: Hodder & Stoughton, 2016).

$\boxed{\text{C}}$ is for Confession

For many people, saying sorry and admitting they got it wrong is really difficult. And yet 'sorry' is one of the most important words to learn and use in life. Good parents know this, teaching their children from a young age the importance of saying 'thank you' (see **G is for Gratitude**), 'please' (see **I is for Intercession**) and this difficult but crucial word – 'sorry'. Similarly if followers of Jesus are to mature we need to learn the importance of saying 'sorry' in prayer to God – what has historically been called *confession*. That's why **C is for Confession**.

When we confess our sins, and mean it, God always forgives us. This is because forgiveness is at the heart of the nature of God.[1] This forgiveness is seen perfectly in the person of Jesus Christ, who died on the cross and rose again in order to win our forgiveness and to welcome us into a living relationship with God. Unlike other religions which say you need to go to a holy man for cleansing every time you've sinned, the Bible tells us to believe in Jesus, our 'great high priest', who on the cross performed the greatest and decisive sacrifice for the sins of all people.[2] So when we put our faith in Christ, we are forgiven for everything we've done wrong. Totally. Utterly. Eternally.

> When we put our faith in Christ, we are forgiven for everything we've done wrong. Totally. Utterly. Eternally.

What a wonderfully loving and forgiving Saviour we have!

For most of us, when we first encounter Jesus and experience his presence and love, we are surprised by his forgiveness. To be in the presence of such love is, for some, quite overwhelming.[3] It often makes people feel dirty and in need of cleansing, which God gladly gives.[4] This initial experience of coming to Christ, of receiving his forgiveness and being filled with his life-giving Spirit is the start of a great adventure of discipleship. The Bible says that our very nature changes from 'sinner' – that is, someone who values independence and whose desires are selfish, to 'saint' – that is, someone who values dependence on Christ and whose desire is to be like him. That doesn't mean that we never do anything wrong again, but it does mean we don't like it. That's why we confess, for we want to become more and more like Jesus. It's what Jesus told his disciples to do, when he taught them to pray daily: 'Forgive us our sins . . .'[5]

This is clearly and succinctly expressed in the Bible by the apostle John, where disciples are told:

> If we confess our sins, [God] is faithful and just and will forgive us our sins and purify us from all unrighteousness . . . My dear children, I write this to you so that you will not sin. But if anybody does sin, we have an advocate with the Father – Jesus Christ, the Righteous One. He is the atoning sacrifice for our sins, and not only ours but also for the sins of the whole world.[6]

My elderly mother, Christine, is in her eighties and has been a believer since making a decision to follow Christ when she was 11 years old. Since then she's developed a close relationship with Jesus and loves praying. Recently she told me that the older she gets the more she's saying 'sorry' to God. This is despite the fact that I, and many others, think my mother is one of the most saintly people we know! So why does she feel the need to confess her sins, and do so regularly? In fact, why do all followers of Christ need to do this? It comes from getting to know God better.

As we get to know God, we realize that he's holy, mighty and good. That he's perfect in love, beauty and majesty. That he's totally trustworthy, caring and kind. That he's always truthful, faithful and forgiving. As we get to know him better and see how amazing he is, we also see that we fall far short of him. We want to say sorry for wrong things in our lives. We want to put things right. Regular confession of sin then becomes something healthy, natural and good, because we don't want anything to spoil our relationship with him, and also we want to be like him. We don't pray confession prayers to earn his love. He loves us anyway! Once we know this, confession then becomes increasingly a response to his goodness, not just constant negativity about our badness.

In some churches, including my own, we offer in most services an opportunity for corporate confession. Together we ask for forgiveness. There are various forms of set words (see **L is for Liturgy**) that can help people confess – on their own behalf or sometimes on behalf of our community or nation too. Then some words of absolution are spoken, declaring God's forgiving love over everyone. By doing this we're not, as occasionally has been suggested, offering people a licence to sin until we gather next time! Rather, we're recognizing the fact that we do sin. And we need to be quick to put things right. Simple as that.

When I confess my sins, my focus is on me and my failings. I say sorry and ask the Holy Spirit to help me to live differently. In doing this I'm intentionally praying about myself. There is nothing wrong with this. In fact, Jesus encouraged us to pray for ourselves[7] – not just prayers of confession, but all sorts of prayers for every circumstance of life. When we do this and pray for ourselves it's often called *supplication*, whereas praying for others is called *intercession* (see **I is for Intercession**).

Sometimes I find that I only recognize my need to confess once I start worshipping God and praying. It's as I draw close to God and realize how good he is, that I'm then convicted of something that I've thought or said or done that was not good. Often this happens in response to adoration (see **A is for Adoration**) as I focus on the greatness and love of God. Conviction – that is, feeling rightly guilty about something that's wrong – is a good thing. The Bible says that the Spirit of God convicts us[8] not to condemn us or make us feel bad about ourselves but because he is for us,[9] and wants us to put things right and live differently. Sometimes when we do wrong, we feel condemned rather than convicted. Condemnation is when we feel shame and think badly not just about what we've done but about ourselves. Condemnation like this never comes from God,[10] but from the devil himself. When we feel condemned and shamed we need to see it for what it is, and rebuke the presence of the evil one. When this happens it's sometimes helpful to have another disciple pray with us that we receive God's loving forgiveness for any wrongdoing, and that we're set free from all sense of shame.

The Bible says that confession can sometimes be done with someone else, with them hearing our confession.[11] I've confessed with others in this way and heard the confessions of lots of people over the years.[12] Sometimes when people confess to me, they think I'll be surprised or disappointed at what they say. To be honest, very little surprises me! I'm usually more touched that they want to be free from guilt and brave enough to share difficult things. Confessing to others is not something we should do with anyone or everyone, but usually with a Christ-follower we honour and trust. In some traditions of the church one of the key roles of the leaders is to hear people's confession and declare over them the forgiveness of Jesus.

There is great power in confession, especially if something has remained unconfessed for a long time. Speaking honestly about our sin (see **H is for Honesty**), sometimes in front of another, can be a liberating and life-changing experience. Sometimes it helps to link confession with fasting (see **F is for Fasting**). By deliberately making my body hungry and showing that I'm not mastered by food, so I'm partnering with the Holy Spirit in not being mastered by sin.

As we receive the Lord's forgiveness, we are washed clean. Thoroughly and entirely. King David knew this about God's forgiveness, writing a whole psalm about it – Psalm 51.

Cleanse me with hyssop, and I will be clean; wash me, and I will be whiter than snow.

Let me hear joy and gladness; let the bones you have crushed rejoice.

Hide your face from my sins and blot out all my iniquity.

Create in me a pure heart, O God, and renew a steadfast spirit within me.

Do not cast me from your presence or take your Holy Spirit from me.

Restore to me the joy of your salvation and grant me a willing spirit, to sustain me.[13]

Followers of Jesus know this joy (see **J is for Joyful**), because Jesus died and rose again for our forgiveness. This forgiveness is activated by confession.

ACTION: Read the story of the two sons in Luke 15:11–32. Which of the two sons do you most identify with? Then look at the father in the story. Look how he forgives and how he speaks to each of his sons and how he treats them. Write down what you notice in the space below or in your notebook.

Are there people who have wronged you whom you need to forgive? If so, write their initials in the space below or in a notebook.

PRAYER: Now begin to pray. Give thanks that God is a forgiving God. Thank Jesus that he died for your forgiveness. If something comes to mind to confess, do it now and receive again his loving-forgiveness.

If there are people whom you need to forgive, ask the Spirit of God to help you and then choose to do that now. (Often we don't feel like forgiving those who've hurt us. Push past that and choose to forgive.) Say to God, 'Lord, I forgive x for what they did to me. I choose to bear no grudges. I forgive them, in Jesus' name.'

Finally, ask for the Lord's help to live as a forgiving person today. To give the benefit of the doubt. To show love and grace, like God.

Further Reading:

Church of England – Common Worship Prayers of Confession and Absolution: http://justus.anglican.org/~ss/commonworship/word/confessions (accessed 7.11.18).

$\boxed{D}$ is for Devotion

I love chatting with Sam, my wife. In the busyness of life I value time when we can be together and share our thoughts, feelings, frustrations and longings. This might be over a coffee at the kitchen table, or as we walk the dog or sometimes over a quiet meal in a restaurant. These times of talking together are crucial to our relationship. But I've also noticed that there are times when it's good to be together when we don't do very much. There's no list of important things to discuss. No agenda. We're just hanging out together. There may be moments when little of great significance is said. Or perhaps much of importance ends up being said. The main thing is being happy and comfortable just being in each other's company.

It's the same in prayer. While it's good to talk to God – and he doesn't mind us bringing a list of things to ask him about (see **I is for Intercession**) – it's also good to have time being in his presence. Enjoying being together. This kind of prayer is sometimes given different names in various traditions, but at its heart it's about appreciating and nurturing our relationship with God, simply for the sake of deepening the relationship. This kind of prayer is deeply devotional. That's why **D is for Devotion**.

Mary of Bethany is a character in the Bible who understood this. She and her family were friends of Jesus, and they loved having him over to their house to stay. There's one occasion when Jesus arrives and Martha, Mary's sister, starts to get a meal ready. Mary, however, just sits at Jesus' feet and enjoys his presence.

Martha continues to be busy with the food preparation whereas Mary doesn't move. She's transfixed with Jesus, to the growing annoyance of Martha. Eventually, Martha can't stand it any more and asks Jesus to get Mary to help her. Here's how Jesus replies:

> Martha, Martha . . . you are worried and upset about many things, but few things are needed – or indeed only one. Mary has chosen what is better, and it will not be taken from her.[1]

It seems that Jesus really values us investing time in getting to know him – more than anything else. It's so easy to get distracted from spending devotional time with Jesus. Like Martha, we get caught up in the busyness of life, even doing good charitable or church-related things for Jesus. We need to learn to choose differently. Mary is an example of someone totally captured by Christ's love. Her eyes were fixed on Jesus!

As we've been learning to pray with our eyes focused on Jesus in our prayer centre in St Cuthbert's House of Prayer in York, so this kind of devotional prayer has become increasingly important. For an activist like me, this doesn't come easily! It's taken a while for many of us to grasp that Jesus not only loves us but really likes us. *He* wants to spend time with *us* – even more than we do with him! We've begun to discover the value of this kind of devotional prayer. After all, what could be better than spending time with God and really getting to know him?

> Jesus not only loves us but really likes us. He wants to spend time with us – even more than we do with him!

Music can aid devotional prayer. Music with words that express love and adoration can be particularly useful, especially as we start our prayers, but it can also be good to use music with no words. This kind of instrumental music – either played by a musician or band, or pre-recorded – can encourage us to focus and, like Mary, to enjoy sitting at Jesus' feet.

There are other times when we simply want to be silent (see **Q is for Quiet**). We want to rest. There are no words. No sounds. No distractions at all except for raw silence. You might daydream or even fall asleep. And that is OK. Because we're in God's presence and seeking him. Seeking his embrace. Seeking greater intimacy. Oswald Chambers (1874–1917) tried to convey something of this when he wrote: 'The idea of prayer is not in order to get answers from God. Prayer is perfect and complete oneness with God.'[2]

We see this desire for devotional prayer beautifully expressed in Psalm 27, which begins with the 'one thing' that Jesus told Martha was needed:

One thing I ask from the LORD, this only do I seek:
that I may dwell in the house of the LORD all the days of my life,
to gaze on the beauty of the LORD and to seek him in his temple . . .
My heart says of you, 'Seek his face!'
Your face, LORD, I will seek.[3]

Interestingly, this prayer-psalm was written by King David during a difficult season in his life when he could easily have allowed fear to dominate his life. Instead of listening to fear he chooses devotional prayer. He knows there's nothing better than resting in God's presence and getting to know the God who loves him. That's why Pete Greig is right when he writes that the value of prayer lies not in 'the power that it releases but the person it reveals.'[4] Devotional prayer reveals Jesus and we are forever changed.

When I think of someone who appreciates this kind of prayer, I think of James Fletcher. James was Head of Prayer at The Belfrey and pioneered and led St Cuthbert's House of Prayer in York for four years until he and his wife, Natasha, moved to Athens to begin a similar work there, working with refugees. As well as leading the team and developing the work of the prayer-house, James spent much time in prayer and worship and learned what it is to sit at Jesus' feet. For James, this wasn't a passive thing but was about being active, seeking to be attentive to all Jesus is saying and doing. James would say this is about an attitude more than an action, where he consciously chooses to practise the presence of God. It was fascinating to see how, over the four years, this changed him. Not only did James grow in his love for Christ and his knowledge of God, but also his leadership gifts massively expanded during those years. When we talked about this before he moved to Athens, James was very humble about it and ended up saying, 'Maybe that's what happens when you spend hours and hours in the presence of God!'

Devotional prayer does require time. It's not the kind of thing you can rush in or out of. But don't let that put you off, if this is new to you. Make some space and have a go, even for a few minutes. Like using a muscle rarely used, it will feel strange at first, but the more you exercise it, the more it will stretch and strengthen, and the easier and more natural it will feel.

This form of prayer is a challenge to busy people. But at the end of the day, all prayer is like that. When I come to pray, there's normally much on my mind and lots of other things I could be doing instead. I've learned that I have to push past all that, and simply start praying. For those who aren't followers of

Jesus and know nothing of the love of Christ and the power of prayer, any kind of prayer – and especially devotional prayer – can seem like futile work. Johannes Hartl, who heads up the Augsburg House of Prayer addresses this so honestly in his wonderful book, *Heart Fire,* when he compares prayer with art, saying: 'Prayer is an art form – a highly demanding art form. Part of what makes art art, is that it is a massive waste of time.'[5] And so it is with prayer.

Devotional prayer is a massive waste of time. And massively worth it.

> Devotional prayer is a massive waste of time. And massively worth it.

ACTION: Read the story of Mary and Martha (in Luke 10:38–42). Write down in the space below or in your notebook what each was doing.

MARY:

MARTHA:

Which of the two do you most identify with? Write down why.

If you are to put into practice this kind of devotional prayer, you will need to make time. In the same way you might fix a time to meet up with a loved-one to eat, or catch up, get out your diary and make an appointment with God, where you intend not just to talk with him, but to hang out with him and rest in his presence. Try to schedule it within the next few days and write it in your diary or on your calendar.

PRAYER: Now begin to pray. Thank the Lord that he really likes you and wants to spend time with you. Ask for his help to do the same.

Read Psalm 27 and make it your prayer – especially verse 4. Tell God that you want to seek him and gaze on his beauty. Ask for the help of the Holy Spirit to grow in this kind of devotional prayer.

Finally, make sure you keep your appointment with God to give time for this. Again, ask the Lord to help and guide you. He will. He loves you and likes you.

Further Reading:

Oswald Chambers, *My Utmost For His Highest* (Grand Rapids, MI: Discovery House, updated 2017).

E is for Extemporary

When it comes to the actual words that we use in prayer to God, there are basically two ways to pray them. One is to use pre-prepared words. These could be my own words that I've already written down – like I might do when I send my wife a card and take care over the words I write. Or they could be words that someone else has written – what is generally called *liturgy* (see **L is for Liturgy**). The other way to pray is to use words that I make up on the spot. They're not pre-prepared. They're not planned. This is how most people pray, most of the time. There's a name for it: it's called *extemporary* prayer. That's why **E is for Extemporary**.

When I talk with people who've just begun following Jesus, I usually suggest that they start praying. They need to begin to talk with God and get the relationship going! What often is said back to me is something like this: 'I don't know where to start. I don't know what to pray. And I don't know if I'll have the right words.' My reply is usually the same: 'Just start. Just start talking to God like you're talking to me. Don't worry about using eloquent words. Just speak from the heart. And when you run out of words, stop.' I know that advice has helped quite a lot of people.

Words are important, but more essential than the actual words that are prayed is the heart behind them. That's true in any relationship. It's possible for me to say lovely words to someone, like 'thank you' or 'I love you' – but not really mean them. It's possible to do the same with God in prayer. While God values our words, he sees beyond them into our hearts. He knows the desires, the motivations and the sentiment behind them. That's why we need to be real and honest in our prayers (see **H is for Honesty**). That's why our prayers need to come from the heart. When we pray like this – usually in an extemporary way – our prayer-words are powerful and transformative.

A great biblical example of someone who prayed extemporary prayers is Moses. When the Lord called him, Moses was not good at speaking. Not to God or to people. He said to God: 'I have never been eloquent, neither in the past nor since you have spoken to your servant. I am slow of speech and tongue' (Exodus 4:10). That's how many of us feel – not just when we're asked to speak publicly to people, but also before God. But Moses learned to speak from the heart in prayer to God and over time they developed a deep and intimate relationship, so much so that later in the story, in Exodus 33, Moses is speaking to God naturally, from the heart. He says things like: 'Teach me your ways so I may know you and continue to find favour with you. Remember that this nation is your people' (v. 13). He also asks God questions, like, 'How will anyone know that you are pleased with me and with your people unless you go with us? What else will distinguish me and your people from all the other people on the face of the earth?' (v. 16). He even prays 'show me your glory' (v. 18). The language is intentionally conversational. It's not formal. It's chatty. It's to the point. It's extemporary.

There's no sense that God is unhappy with this form of prayer spoken by Moses. Far from it, he seems to like it, so much so that he responds and speaks back – you can read all about it in Exodus 33! The way the writer of Exodus summarizes it is like this: 'The LORD would speak to Moses face to face, as one speaks to a friend' (v. 11). If that is how the Lord spoke with Moses, who was not able to know God as intimately as we can as followers of Jesus, how much more can we pray our extemporary prayers and know God's voice. It comes out of honest, real extemporary prayer.

Something else we notice from the story of Moses is that God speaks his language! In the same way that Moses speaks to God using his ordinary, everyday language, so God speaks to him in the same way. Because God knows all things and knows us, he knows our language. I only speak one language – English – so he speaks to me in English. He does this as I read a Bible translated into English, and also he speaks into my mind and heart in English, as I pray. If I was Italian, he'd speak in Italian. If I was Japanese, he'd speak in Japanese. While we value the original languages in which the Bible was written – which are mainly Hebrew for the Old Testament and Greek for the New Testament – followers of Jesus do not believe, lil some religions, that there is one holy language that God prefers to speak in. When God came in Christ to show us his love, he deeply embedded himself in the culture of the day and spoke the local language. It's the same today. We don't have to learn Hebrew, Greek (or Latin) to pray. We just pray. With our heart-language.[1] It's called extemporary prayer.

Sophie Dearden, who now heads up St Cuthbert's House of Prayer in York is a bright, bubbly, bold prayer warrior in her late twenties. I love to hear her extemporary prayers and say a good *Amen* ('let it be') at the end! When she leads us in prayer she speaks to the Lord from the heart, with lovely, honest, heartfelt prayers. She is reverent yet real. Bold but not brash. Strong yet sensitive. Although some might see her as rather young to lead, she's actually been following Jesus most of her life and so her public extemporary praying is a simple expression of many years of privately praying like that just between her and God. She's learned to talk to God, from the heart, with love and passion.

The more we pray extemporary prayers to God, the easier and more natural they become. If you're new to this and have never heard anyone pray extemporaneously, you might be taken aback by the way they pray. But actually all they're doing is just talking with God, like they might talk with you, using their ordinary, everyday language.

It can sometimes help to have a simple prayer structure to use as a springboard to help extemporary prayer. For example, many use *The Lord's Prayer*,[2] starting and ending with adoration and covering four main sections in-between:

Adoration: 'Our Father in heaven, hallowed be your name,'
1) *Intercession:* 'your kingdom come, your will be done, on earth as in heaven.'
2) *Provision:* 'Give us today our daily bread.'
3) *Confession:* 'Forgive us our sins as we forgive those who sin against us.'
4) *Guidance:* 'Lead us not into temptation but deliver us from evil.'
Adoration: 'For the kingdom, the power, and the glory are yours now and for ever.'

Others use the simple three-fold structure of: *thank you, sorry, please*:

Thank you: Giving thanks for God's goodness, expressed in so many ways
Sorry: Looking back and putting anything right with God
Please: Asking God for anything you need

My grandfather, Luther Porter, prayed similar extemporary prayers. His day job was selling crockery on Doncaster market, but his passion was prayer and evangelism. When he prayed out loud, hearts were stirred. He sometimes wept as he prayed, recognizing the deep love of God, and wanting to see the Lord move in power and change lives. Grandpa Luther learned to pray from Samuel Chadwick. Samuel Chadwick was principal of Cliff College in the 1920s and my grandfather studied under him. In fact, one day, when carrying out the early morning task of delivering the daily post, Luther stopped outside Chadwick's office, hearing the sound of the man praying behind the closed door. He loved to hear him pray, so Luther paused and bent down with his ear to the keyhole to listen to the prayers of the man of God. Luther later told his son, my father, what happened next.

> The praying stopped [so] he listened more intently until the door suddenly opened.
>
> 'What are you doing there, Brother Porter?'
>
> Dumbfounded and embarrassed he rose to his feet.
>
> 'Come inside.'
>
> There on the desk was a list of students' names, and Mr Chadwick was praying for each one by name.
>
> 'Let's see. Where's your name?'
>
> He ran his finger down the page.
>
> 'Right, Brother Porter. I can see we're going to have to pray very hard for you!'[3]

Samuel Chadwick went on to write a classic book on prayer called *The Path of Prayer*. In it he says that this kind of extemporary prayer is 'the prayer that prevails' and 'is personal, intimate, and original'.[4] It comes from the heart. That's why

Johannes Hartl is right when he says 'there is no correct form of prayer'.[5] Some disciples need to be less concerned about getting the words exactly right and instead just start talking to God. Maybe that's why Jesus tells us to be child-like when we approach God in prayer.[6] Children just say it as it is. There's no script. No show. No pretence. No fear. That's how disciples are to come to God in prayer, as we speak from the heart our extemporary prayers.

> Jesus tells us to be child-like when we approach God in prayer. Children just say it as it is. There's no script. No show. No pretence. No fear.

ACTION: From the earliest days, people have talked to God, using their heart-language. For example, we read in Genesis 4:26 that 'people began to call on the name of the LORD'. Look back on your life. Can you recall the first time you ever prayed a prayer that was extemporary – from the heart? If not, recall a more recent one. Write it down in the space below or in your notebook.

Now take a closer look at the prayer you've just written. Why did you pray that prayer? What was really on your heart? How did it feel to pray like that?

If you are someone who finds it hard to pray extemporary prayers in front of others, why not resolve to say 'grace' before you eat with other people? Just a sentence or two is needed. Not only will it point to Christ (and perhaps be a topic of conversation with those with whom you're eating), but it can be a place where you can learn to pray naturally from the heart.

PRAYER: Ask the Lord to help you grow in extemporary prayer. Then take three situations (for example, the three named below) and begin to talk to the Lord about each one. Tell him what's on your heart for these situations. Let passion arise for them, as you begin to call on God and ask him to move and bring his love and power.

1) A situation in the world.
2) A situation at home or work.
3) A situation personal to you.

End by thanking him for his presence, praying that you will keep talking with him from the heart through the day.

Further Reading:

Samuel Chadwick, *The Path of Prayer* (London: Hodder & Stoughton; Independent: CrossReach Publications, 1931, 2017).

$\boxed{F}$ is for Fasting

Fasting is the *voluntary giving up of food*.[1] It's choosing not to eat, allowing ourselves to get hungry, so we can then channel that hunger in prayer. We let our bodies get hungry, so that we hunger for God. Fasting is an ancient spiritual discipline, practised by many people in the Bible, including Jesus himself. Jesus taught his followers to fast,[2] seeing it as basic and essential to discipleship. That's why this short book on prayer devotes a whole chapter to fasting and why **F is for Fasting**.

Barney has been a follower of Jesus for a while, although in recent years he and his wife have been going on a fresh adventure with Christ. They're discovering there's a whole lot more to discipleship than they realized. Barney and I were chatting in a coffee shop recently when he told me that having read my book *A–Z of Discipleship* some months previously, there were now two things he and his wife, Sheila, were doing that they weren't before. One was getting up early to pray. The other was fasting. They were now fasting one day every week, as part of their regular rhythm of prayer, as well as doing occasional fasts too. Later, he went on to tell me how, since then, God had seemed to answer their prayers for a number of situations, and that his sister, for whom they'd been praying for some time, had now recommitted her life to Jesus. I encouraged them to keep going, and not be afraid to pray bold, brave prayers as they pray and fast.

Prayer can never be proved. What seems like an answer to prayer could of course have happened through some other means, or just been a fluke.[3] Prayer with fasting is the same. Barney could not tell me that their answered prayers were due in whole or part to prayer and fasting, although I suspect they were! That's because I've been around people who pray and fast for long enough to know that when we do that, things happen. That's why I sometimes say that fasting releases God's power. Because it does. It unleashes exponential energy and resources greater than the effort put in. Most of the saints of old knew this, with the fourth-century church leader Basil the Great summarizing much of their teaching when he wrote: 'Fasting gives birth to prophets and strengthens the powerful; fasting makes lawgivers wise. Fasting is a good safeguard for the soul, a steadfast companion for the body, a weapon for the valiant, and a gymnasium for athletes. Fasting repels temptations, anoints unto piety; it is the comrade of watchfulness and the artificer of chastity. In war it fights bravely, in peace it teaches stillness.'[4]

> Fasting unleashes exponential energy and resources greater than the effort put in.

Church leader and Bible teacher John Mark Comer gives three helpful reasons for fasting: to starve the flesh to feed the spirit, to pray and to identify with the poor.[5] As such, fasting is an expression of humble prayer.[6] Disciples of Jesus do this not so much to get God to act, but more in response to something.[7] That 'something' might be a crisis event, or a sin committed (see **C is for Confession**) or an inaction, like Barney's family member who was not following Jesus. Some fast because they recognize they need a great hunger for God. That's why fasting is often linked with prayer for change. We're not satisfied with the ways things are, so we fast. And instead of eating, we pray. And as we feel the hunger pangs, we pray. In the Bible we see people fasting in response to: an uncertain journey ahead;[8]

a sin committed;[9] death;[10] when feeling unsafe;[11] when lacking direction;[12] when ill;[13] when choosing leaders;[14] when a spiritual battle is coming;[15] when a national disaster is coming;[16] when feeling spiritually hungry;[17] when seeking to grow in holiness.[18]

This means that fasting is not about twisting God's arm. As Bill Johnson says: 'Fasting is not a hunger strike. It is not a time when we let God know what we want and threaten not to eat until we get it. That would be manipulation . . . True fasting is when we hunger for God's world more than we hunger for this one.'[19] It's part of praying what Jesus told his disciples to pray in *The Lord's Prayer:* that God's kingdom – his rule and reign – would come here on earth as in heaven.

When we fast, we channel hunger into prayer. In doing so, we find ourselves more body-aware. More in touch with our bodies. This is a good thing. The natural rhythm of eating three meals a day, although not bad, is rarely challenged in western culture. So when we get hungry, we eat. But when we fast we challenge this normal routine. We say to our bodies that we're not going to be mastered by physical hunger.[20] If you've never done this, it will feel strange and uncomfortable at first. If you usually drink coffee you're likely to get headaches for a day or so as the caffeine leaves your body. But the more you do it, the easier it gets, so much so that seasoned fasters look forward to it! They know it's good for them – for their soul and body – but most importantly, it's effective. Things change. This doesn't mean that every prayer prayed while fasting is answered as we'd like. It just means that more prayers seem to get answered. Indeed, Jesus taught and modelled this, telling his disciples who were struggling to free a boy from demonic oppression that 'This kind can come out only by prayer and fasting'.[21]

Most fasts are short – maybe missing a meal or fasting from sunrise to sunset. Normally we keep drinking water but stop everything else. Sometimes you can fast for longer – for a weekend or a few days. Fasting is meant for healthy adults and fine in short doses for pregnant women, but shouldn't be imposed on babies, young children or the elderly or frail. Fasting normally involves making space and slowing down from the normal pace of life. Care should be taken when fasting, especially if you make little or no adjustment to a fast-paced schedule. If others in your house are not fasting, this should be respected, with the Bible saying we shouldn't make a show of this kind of prayer.[22]

I try to fast as a regular part of my weekly rhythm of prayer. I also fast at particular times and seasons. I think this mix of regular and occasional fasting is good, and follows the teaching and practice of the Christ-followers of the early years of the church – the Early Church Fathers – as well as the pattern of many revivalists, such as the first Methodists. If you're new to fasting, just start (unless there's a medical reason why you shouldn't). Set a date and time and miss a meal, and use the time to pray. Begin to practise. As you do that, and push past some of the initial hunger pangs, you'll begin to see the benefit of praying whilst fasting.

Fasting, however, does not work in some circumstances. The Bible is clear that it can lose its power and effectiveness if we don't love people. If we oppress people, treating them unkindly and instead exploit them, then God says our fasting prayers become null and void. This is the message of Isaiah 58, which is all about effective fasting. God tells his people that their fasting has to be combined with living justly. It's no good fasting mechanically. Fasting isn't a divine slot machine that automatically produces the jackpot, irrespective to the lifestyle of the people fasting. Rather, it's part of the prayer armoury of devoted, humble disciples who love God and love people and want to see God's kingdom come – the kingdom where there is no sickness, sin or suffering. If we forget this, then fasting can become legalistic and unhelpful. If we remember this and practise this, then fasting will change us and the way we live, and our prayers will be modelled in our lifestyle.

Fasting has been a much-neglected form of prayer in much of the Western Church over the last few generations. It's time we discovered why Jesus said 'when you fast' to his disciples, not 'if' you fast.[23] It's one of the best ways that disciples and leaders grow in their relationship with God, as they learn to trust him, pray to him and see his power released in the world. Maybe Mark Batterson is correct when he says that: 'An empty stomach may be the most powerful prayer posture in Scripture.'[24]

ACTION: Read Acts 13:1–3. This describes the dynamic church in Antioch. Do a short Bible study on this passage, answering the following questions:

What, according to verse 2, was the church doing when they gathered?

What, according to verse 2, did the Holy Spirit do in response?

What does verse 3 say the disciples then did?

What do we learn about fasting from this passage?

When was the last time you fasted and prayed? If you've never done that – or not for a while – get your diary/calendar and schedule a time to miss a meal (this week if possible, while it's fresh on your mind). Resolve to use that time to respond to something on your heart. As you do that, make sure you pray, read the Bible and listen to God. Also, listen to your body and its hunger for food. Turn that into a desire to hunger for God. Tell him you want more of him. Begin to learn to fast.

PRAYER: Ask the Lord to teach you about fasting and how to hunger more for him. If you ask, he will increase this desire. Start today.

Worship and adore him for who he is and what he's done. Give him your love and adoration. As you do this, be open to him bringing to mind a few circumstances out of which it would be good to pray and fast.

Finally, ask him to connect you with another follower of Jesus who is learning about fasting, so you can share experiences and grow together in this lovely and powerful form of prayer.

Further Reading:

Arthur Wallis, *God's Chosen Fast* (Sandycroft: CLC International, 1968, 2015).

G is for Gratitude

Students at the school I went to in my teenage years were required to attend a gathering on a Wednesday morning called 'assembly'. This would involve the singing of a hymn, a word of moral encouragement and some notices. It would always close with a prayer, normally led by the head teacher. At the end of each term, he would often read the same prayer from his old prayerbook, introducing it as the *General Thanksgiving*.[1] It got my attention, not just because he was using the same prayer again but because the more I heard it prayed, the more I appreciated it. There was something about it that was compelling. I wasn't sure at the time exactly what it was, but I knew it had something to do with the sense of thankfulness behind all the words and phrases. To be thankful to God and to others felt important. Since then I've discovered much more about prayer, and about the crucial place of thanksgiving. I now know that what was attracting me was the attitude of gratitude.

Gratitude is about being thankful. Grateful. Appreciative. And then expressing that in word and action. Gratitude is an essential part of prayer. That's why **G is for Gratitude.**

Gratitude has always been important for followers of Jesus, modelled beautifully in a story told in Luke 17:11–19 of a Samaritan man who was healed by Jesus.[2] This man was one of nine others who had a skin disease called leprosy. They probably lived together in community, in isolation from the rest of the village. When Jesus passed through their neighbourhood, we're told that the ten lepers called out to him, from a distance, saying 'Jesus, Master, have pity on us!' They were asking Jesus to heal them, in the same way that many do today in prayer. Jesus told them to go and show themselves to the priest – the one in the community who could pronounce whether their skin disease was gone or not – and as they went on their way, their skin disease was healed. You can imagine their joy! Not only were they well, but now they were no longer social pariahs. They could rejoin society and their families. They could work and make a living. Not just their bodies but their very lives were restored! That could have been the end of the story, but Luke goes on, focusing on one of the ten men. 'One of them', he says, 'when he saw he was healed, came back, praising God in a loud voice. He threw himself at Jesus' feet and thanked him . . . ' This man took the time to go back and express his gratitude to Jesus, something the other nine forgot to do.

It's easy to forget to be thankful. This can be the case whatever is going on in our lives. For instance, we can forget to be thankful when life seems to be going wrong. If our focus is on difficult circumstances and on the size of our problems – rather than the size of our God – then we may forget to pray thankful prayers. But this can be the case too when life is going well! Which is why Jesus says to the cleansed leper who came back to him: 'Were not all ten cleansed? Where are the other nine?' That's why disciples need to know that the attitude of gratitude is not dependent on circumstances (see **J is for Joyful**). Rather, we can pray thanksgiving prayers any time, any place, anywhere. That's why the Bible says 'give thanks in all circumstances'.[3]

> The attitude of gratitude is not dependent on circumstances. Rather, we can pray thanksgiving prayers any time, any place, anywhere.

We don't give thanks *for* every circumstance. There are many things in life that are not good and we want to see changed, and it's good and right that we pray that they do (see **I is for Intercession**). But *in* every circumstance we are to give thanks. We see this in the way the first followers of Jesus prayed after Peter and John had been arrested and told not to speak about Jesus (in Acts 4:23–31). We're told that the church gathered and prayed. What did they do first? They prayed prayers of adoration (see **A is for Adoration**) and thanksgiving, before then asking God to embolden them to defy the authorities and speak and heal in the name of Jesus. They gave thanks.

When I think of someone praying prayers of gratitude, I think of Roger Simpson. Roger was the vicar of St Michael le Belfrey before me, and I came to work with him, before we swapped jobs. Roger is a gifted evangelist and Bible teacher, with a great big heart for people. One of the first things I noticed about him was that when he led us in prayer, he'd always get us to give thanks before we interceded and asked for anything. Sometimes he would urge us to go on with our prayers of thanksgiving – not to stop too early. He would often say 'there is so much to be thankful for' and he was right. And then, of course, he lived this in his life – often going round encouraging and thanking people.

In the middle of the Bible we find the book of Psalms. Originally the hymn-book of the Jerusalem temple, we no longer have the music, but we do have the words. The Psalms are so helpful for prayer and worship. Not only do they help us pray, but being part of God's inspired word in the Bible they give us confidence when we pray, helping us to know the kind of prayers God loves to receive. And one of the key themes in the Psalms is gratitude. It comes through again and again. In fact one of the most common refrains in the Psalms is this: 'Give thanks to the LORD, for he is good; his love endures for ever.'[4] This reminds us that saying 'thank you' to God is not just a good thing to do, it's what we're called to do. That's because the created should always give thanks to the Creator. The healed should always give thanks to the Healer. The saved should always give thanks to the Saviour.

But also, it's good for us to give thanks. Research shows that thankful people are happier and healthier than others, and that thankful people are good to be around. We all love to hang out with encouraging, thankful people! Moaners and groaners can drain the life out of us. But grateful people lift our souls and gladden our hearts.

I was recently at a Christian festival and found myself standing in quite a long coffee queue waiting to place my order. The people serving were all volunteers and were busy, working hard and processing the orders. There was much demand and everyone was hoping to get their drink before the meeting started. When I got to the front of the queue I ordered my coffee and cake-of-the-day and thanked the woman who took my order. I also thanked the man who cut my slice of cake, telling him I was grateful for the way he was looking after us all in this practical way. At that point, the woman in front of me, with whom I'd chatted briefly whilst standing in the queue, turned to me and spoke, saying something I wasn't expecting. She looked at me and smiled and said: 'You understand grace.' And then she said it again, 'You understand grace.' She then walked off to pay. I was surprised and struck by her comment, connecting gratitude and grace. It got me thinking.

Gratitude is thankfulness. Grace is love. Grace is the amazing love of God which is unconditional, undeserved and unending.

Grace is seen perfectly in the person of Jesus Christ and explained to us in the pages of the Bible. So I suspect the woman was trying to say that a life touched by grace should be a life marked by gratitude, and I think she's right. That being the case, I know I still have much to discover of God's grace.

When we experience God's grace – then what can we do but be thankful? Thankful to God in lifestyle, and thankful to God in our prayers. It's an expression of gratitude for all his love, goodness and provision.

Many of us subliminally believe we live in a world of not enough. Where we're not good enough, not able enough and where we don't have enough. But once we experience the grace of God in Jesus Christ, we're given a very different narrative. Grace is about *more than enough*. Ann Voskamp has penned some of the most helpful and profound words about gratitude in recent years. Writing about thanksgiving in the midst of the joys and struggles of life, she says this as she reflects on how Jesus gives thanks before he feeds 5,000 people from five loaves and two fish:

> The real problem of life is never a lack . . .
> The real problem of life – *in my life* – is lack of thanksgiving.
> Thanksgiving creates abundance; and the miracle of multiplying happens when I give thanks.[5]

The apostle Paul urged the church in Philippi to: 'Be saturated in prayer throughout each day, offering your faith-filled requests before God with overflowing gratitude.'[6] So learn to pray prayers of gratitude. *Thank you* prayers. Not only does it please God, but it will change your heart, your outlook and those around you.

ACTION: Think of the last time you expressed thanks to someone and it had a positive reaction. When was it? What did you say? What was the reaction? Write below, or in your notebook, a summary.

Think of a time recently when someone thanked you for something, and it stirred you. What did they say? How did it move you? Write it down below or in your notebook.

Now write below, or in your notebook, five things for which you are grateful to God today.

PRAYER: Read Psalm 100 – subtitled in many English Bible translations as 'For giving grateful praise.' Speak the words out loud as a prayer and then begin to use your own words to give thanks to God. Make sure you express gratitude for the five things listed above. If you can, keep going and let thanksgiving arise from your heart as you recognize the goodness of the Lord.

En by praying that you will be a person of thanksgiving today – giving thanks to God as you go through the day, and also thanking people around you for what they do and who they are.

Further Reading:

Ann Voskamp, *One Thousand Gifts* (Grand Rapids, MI: Zondervan, 2010).

H is for Honesty

Gratitude and praise, as we've been discovering, are an important part of prayer (see **G is for Gratitude**). We often sing songs at our church telling God that our lives are open to him and that nothing is concealed. I like that, because it reminds us that God knows, sees and hears everything. Not just the good, but the bad. Not just the tidy, but the messy. Not just the clean, but the dirty. And yet he still bids us to come to him. So we need to come as we are and be real when we pray. There's no place for pretence. True prayer involves taking off our masks and being vulnerable and open before God. That's why, when it comes to prayer, **H is for Honesty**.

> True prayer involves taking off our masks and being vulnerable and open before God.

When I pray, God desires to see the real me. The nineteenth-century Scottish minister Robert Murray M'Cheyne, who was a poet and deep man of prayer, summarized it like this: 'A man is what he is on his knees before God – nothing more.'[1] True, effective praying begins with us showing God our true selves, as we talk with him about our lives and our world – the good, the bad and the ugly.

I've known Steve for almost twenty years. I first met him and his wife, Joy, in Sheffield when I was vicar of St Chad's Church in Woodseats. I liked him from the start, because there was an honesty and openness about him that was disarming. Steve's always had a passion for justice and for people who are struggling and caught up in poverty. That's why I encouraged him to set up Besom in Sheffield, which creates a bridge between those who have and those who don't. When he took early retirement, I brought Steve onto the church staff team and we got to know each other well. Even though we now live in different cities we still meet up regularly, and when we meet we always pray. When Steve prays, I often smile, because he just says it as it is. He's always done that, especially when things aren't going well or particular provision is needed from the Lord. He just tells him. 'Lord, we need your help' is a prayer Steve often prays. And he prays it from the heart. With honesty. When I think of honest prayer, I think of Steve.

Sometimes when I pray, asking for God's help in all sorts of situations, I imagine a big table – the kind you might find in a good-sized dining room. I imagine myself getting out all sorts of bits of paper – which represent the things I want to talk to God about – and I lay them all out on the table for the Lord to see. He knows about them anyway, but I expose them to him, so he and I can clearly see what's on my heart. Maybe this was the kind of thing that King David had in mind when he tells God in Psalm 5: 'I lay my requests before you.'[2] Jesus urges us to pray and worship like this, telling us to 'worship . . . in truth'.[3] When Paul tells the church in Ephesus they should be 'speaking the truth in love' to one another,[4] he could just as well be writing about prayer, as we speak to God in the same way. This is because, as Psalm 139 makes patently clear, God knows everything about each one of us, and loves us. He wants the best for us and for our world, and even thinks amazing thoughts about us![5]

So we pray about the good things. But we bring him the difficult things too. The brokenness of the world. The pain of fractured relationships. The selfishness that exploits. The healings that don't seem to be happening. The struggles and sins. The frustrations and fears. We tell God, in honesty, not just about things 'out there in the world' such as social unrest and famines, but things close to home, in our workplace, our family, our life. We need to be honest.

Some find this difficult because of a wrong understanding of God and prayer. Author Jim Manney admits to this, saying: 'For years I had a terrible time praying because I thought that prayer was for good people. I prayed when I felt virtuous; I avoided it when I felt guilty or ashamed or defeated, which meant that I didn't pray much for long stretches. I eventually realized that it was OK to be honest with God.'[6]

God loves our honest prayers. He doesn't mind us praying for ourselves. It's not wrong or selfish to do this. He wants us to pray for what we need and in the same way that a loving parent loves to provide for their child and doesn't mind their children asking, so the Lord likes to give us good things too. This is not to encourage us to be greedy, rather it's to help us see how good and kind and generous he is. We see this in the famous prayer of Jabez, in 1 Chronicles 4:10, where Jabez prays:

'Oh, that you would bless me and enlarge my territory! Let your hand be with me, and keep me from harm so that I will be free from pain.' And God granted his request.

God also doesn't mind us telling him when we find it hard to pray, or even that there are times when we don't really want to pray at all. He is big enough to cope with such transparency.

God loves to help us and to answer our honest prayers, although he may not always answer them as we want (see **U is for**

Unanswered). It's really hard when God seems silent. What do I do? Or when it feels like the answer from God is 'no' but I so desperately want it to be 'yes'. How should I pray? It starts by me telling God all about it. Sharing my heart with him. Being vulnerable about my dilemmas and doubts. Pouring out my honest prayers to him.

We see this in the Bible in the prayers of Job. His life seems to fall apart, as his family die, his business fails and his health deteriorates. Yet he is honest with the Lord about everything that is going on, somehow being able to find faith to trust God in the midst of deep pain.

We see this too in the prayers of Hezekiah. Hezekiah was king of Judah in the eighth century BC during a time of political unrest as Assyria, under the leadership of King Sennacherib, sought to sweep up nearby nations into its brutal empire. According to 2 Kings 19 this all came to a head as a huge Assyrian army gathered near Jerusalem ready to attack. Hezekiah is buoyed by a prophetic word from Isaiah, but nevertheless the situation looks dire, especially as he receives a letter of ultimatum from the Assyrians. So what does Hezekiah do? We're told that 'he went up to the temple of the LORD and spread [the letter] out before the LORD'. Like David in Psalm 5, he doesn't hide the situation from God but rather gets it out in the open. Then he prays. He starts with adoration (see **A is for Adoration**) – 'LORD, the God of Israel, enthroned between the cherubim'[7] and then turns to gratitude (see **G is for Gratitude**) for what God has done – 'You have made heaven and earth'[8] – before quickly turning to the issue at hand, praying, 'Give ear, LORD, and hear; open your ears, LORD, and see; listen to the words Sennacherib has sent to ridicule the living God.'[9] Hezekiah is honest with God about the power of the enemy army and of their past record, saying 'It is true, LORD, that the Assyrian kings have laid waste these nations and their lands'[10] but he's brave and bold in asking for help. He prays: 'Now, LORD our God, deliver us from his hand'.[11] We then read of how God remarkably intervened and answered Hezekiah's prayer – and no doubt the prayers of many others being prayed at that time too – with a mighty deliverance! Hezekiah is not presented as a perfect king, but he does know about prayer, and how it's important to pray honest prayers.

I keep a journal, where I record my thoughts and reflections about life. I write about significant milestones in life, note prophecies and also write some of my prayers. Sometimes these are big faith-filled prayers (see **V is for Vision**), but I also try to record things I'm struggling with, expressing my honest prayers in written form. It's often a very helpful thing to do, allowing me to articulate on paper how I feel to God. It's a useful and a different way of praying, especially when life is tough.

Honest prayers, however, are not just for the difficult times, or for a crisis. We're supposed to pray with honesty and integrity all the time (see **R is for Relentless**). We can pray like this about everything. About big things and little things. And we can ask for God's help in all sorts of situations, and for all kinds of people. No one has modelled this better for me than Margaret Ludlam, who was an elderly lady who came every week to our church prayer meeting in Sheffield and loved praying honest prayers for the ordinary things of life. She gave thanks for the people who helped children cross busy roads, and asked God to give them a good break during school holidays. She prayed that the local police officers would be kept safe and solve crime. She prayed for shopkeepers and for their businesses to thrive as they served the community well. I loved hearing Margaret's honest prayers for all kinds of people, and I expect she's continuing to pray them now in heaven!

Praying with honesty is essentially about being real before God. At the most basic level this is about recognizing our need for him and telling him. It's OK to pray like this for ourselves. And as we do this, we need again and again to be filled with his presence and love. That's why the prayer 'Come Holy Spirit' is a good one! We need him. I need him. You need him. So be honest, and tell him. He loves our honest prayers.

ACTION: How honest are you, when you pray? Do you tell God what is troubling you, as well as what is encouraging you? If not, why not? (You might like to write your reflections in the space below or in your notebook.)

Is there an honest prayer you need to be praying today – maybe about a situation in your life or that of your loved ones? So you don't forget it, write below or in your notebook a few words to remind you about it for when you come to pray.

PRAYER: Think about people you know who model honesty before God in prayer. Give thanks for them. Ask the Lord to help you become even more honest in your prayers.

Now pick up the situation you noted above, and begin to talk to the Lord about it. Tell him how it is. How it makes you feel. What is good and what is not. Ask for him to help and intervene. Pray for his kingdom of love, joy and peace to come.

End by praying that you'll be a person of honesty and integrity today. Ask that your honesty before God would express itself in honest dealings with people, as you speak the truth in love.

Further Reading:

William P. Young, *The Shack* (London: Hodder & Stoughton, 2008).

$\boxed{\text{I}}$ is for Intercession

When most people think about prayer, they think about asking God for things. As we've been seeing in this book, prayer is much broader than that. At its heart, prayer is about having an ongoing relationship with God. It's about knowing him in Jesus Christ – and getting to know him more through conversation. It's about adoration and gratitude and confession and much more – and doing so using our heart-language in an open and honest way. But prayer also *does* include asking God for things, both for ourselves and for others. In fact, it's a good and important part of prayer which mustn't be neglected. Praying in this way for ourselves is often called *supplication* while praying like this for others is known as *intercession*. That's why **I is for Intercession**.

One picture of intercession is that of someone standing in a gap. On one side of the gap is heaven, the dwelling-place of God where he and all the infinite resources of his kingdom reside. On the other side is earth, which to some extent lacks God's presence and the resources of heaven. When we intercede, we stand in the gap and pray for God's kingdom to come on earth as in heaven. When we pray in this way, we're mirroring one of the important roles of a *priest* in the Old Testament, who would do two main things: 1) offer sacrifices and 2) pray to God on behalf of people. Since the coming of Christ, no more sacrifices need to be offered, as our Lord became the ultimate sacrifice through his death, paying once and for all the price for our sins.[1] When Jesus did this, he stood in the gap, bridging heaven and earth and so became our 'great high priest'.[2] So the first function of a priest is finished – fully achieved by Christ. But Jesus continues in the second role, now sitting at God's right hand in heaven, interceding. As his followers we are called to follow him and be people of prayer, interceding like him for all sorts of people and places. Banning Liebscher, founder and leader of Jesus Culture puts it like this: 'The Head Intercessor who lives to make intercession for us has invited us in to join with Him as He intercedes. Can you think of anything better than partnering with Jesus to see the dreams of His heart realized?'[3]

The Bible tells us to ask in intercession. For example, when the senior leader Paul gives instruction to the junior leader Timothy about prayer, he says: 'pray with gratitude to God. Pray for all men with all forms of prayers and requests as you intercede with intense passion. And pray for every political leader and representative . . .'[4]

So all followers of Jesus are called to intercede. We must pray for the world, for the church and for situations around us. We can do this on our own, but there's great benefit in doing so with others. That's why it's good to gather regularly with a small or larger group to intercede. Some meet in twos or threes to support each other and to intercede for particular issues. In addition to all the prayer going on in St Cuthbert's House of Prayer, at The Belfrey we have an early morning prayer meeting once a week where we worship and then intercede for lots of different things. Those leading guide us to pray, sometimes giving information or introducing people who we then pray for. Ending with breakfast as we go into our day, this prayer meeting is the most important regular meeting in the life of our church. We also meet three times a year in the evening as a whole church to intercede, pausing our midweek groups so we can come together and pray. These meetings are very important to us, as we unite as a church to intercede.

Having said this, some also value interceding on their own. This includes those who know they're particularly called to be intercessors. Such people know it's their main role in God's family, feeling called to give significant time to it. In every generation God has raised up people like this. Many of them have been part of the monastic tradition[5] in the church. Some today are part of the Houses of Prayer[6] and 24/7 Prayer[7] movements that continue to grow. In the Bible, Anna is such a character. She was a gifted prophet, which means she heard from God and often spoke his words into people's lives. She dedicated her life to being in God's temple where we're told: 'She . . . worshipped night and day, fasting and praying.'[8] As an elderly lady she was given the privilege before she died of meeting the baby Jesus as his parents brought him into the temple, and as a result she 'gave thanks . . . and spoke about the child to all'.[9]

When we come to intercede, there are many things we could pray for. Sometimes it's hard to know where to start, but don't let that put you off. What's most important is to start somewhere. So just start praying! Sometimes I find it helpful to have a simple structure, like: *pray globally; pray nationally; pray locally*. I might focus on the persecuted church, perhaps using material produced by organisations supporting Christ-followers in very difficult parts of the world. Sometimes when we pray in church we pray for issues in the news or issues that are especially influencing our locality. As we do this, we need to be aware that so much of the news that is fed to us today is driven by a bad news agenda.

This bad news culture can sometimes skew our intercessions in a certain direction and can also rub off on those called to intercede. To ensure that we pray, as the Bible says, 'according to [God's] will',[10] it's important that our intercessions are informed most of all by Scripture, as we allow God's word to shape our prayers. So when we come to intercede it's good to ask God to direct our praying. He loves to do this, and will bring Bible passages to mind, and often give us words and pictures and other prophecies (see **P is for Prophetic**) to guide our praying. Beni Johnson writes about this in her helpful book, *The Happy Intercessor,* saying that the attitude behind much contemporary intercession is 'praying out of fear. Prayers that are fear-based are not prayers that will produce a heavenly answer . . . Instead, we need to make sure that we remain focused on God and on what He is doing. The key is to always ask God, "Father, what are you doing?"'[11] and then pray in the light of that. Interceding in this way picks up the strategy of Jesus, who said he only '[does] what he sees his Father doing'.[12]

When I think of intercession, I think of Lou Engle, founder of The Call. The Call was a prayer movement in the USA which began in 1999, calling America to turn back to God. I've never met Lou personally, but I've heard him speak a few times. I know he's a passionate person of prayer, and has a lovely way of encouraging those around him to pray. Lou often talks about his weaknesses, how he sometimes finds intercession hard and that he has to keep learning the importance of perseverance. But he keeps going because he truly believes that we change history through prayer. We see this in the Bible in the way Abraham prayed for the city of Sodom.[13] Abraham talked to God and God with him, and Abraham interceded for the city, finally getting God to agree to change his plans if he could find ten righteous people in the city. This Old Testament story raises all sorts of fascinating questions about the plans and purposes of God, showing most importantly that God listens as we intercede. He hears our prayers. Our intercessions really do make a difference!

> God listens as we intercede. He hears our prayers. Our intercessions really do make a difference!

As we intercede, we can be motivated not just by Abraham but by lots of biblical forerunners. These include: Jacob, who wrestled in prayer all night and sought God's blessing (Gen. 32:22–30); Moses, who lay prostrate in intercession for God's people (Deut. 9:25–27); Ezekiel, who stood 'in the gap' between earth and heaven when no one else could be found (Ezek. 22:30); and Daniel, who knelt three times a day in prayer for his home city (Dan. 6:10). Today, Jesus intercedes on behalf of all 'who come to God through him' (Heb. 7:25).

As we intercede, we can pray in all kinds of ways. We can speak our prayers. Shout our prayers. Sing our prayers. Draw our prayers. Write down our prayers. Symbolise our prayers. Walk out our prayers. And much more.

The important thing is to pray. To ask. To stand in the gap and intercede.

Some are afraid to ask. What if God doesn't answer? How bold and brave should I be? How long should I go on for? These questions and more are learned as we pray. That's why the advice I always give to people is this: just do it. Make a start. As Samuel Chadwick said: 'There is no way to learn to pray but by praying. No reasoned philosophy of prayer ever taught a soul to pray. The subject is beset with problems, but there are no problems of prayer to the man who prays. They are all met in the fact of answered prayer and the joy of fellowship with God.'[14]

ACTION: Having read this chapter, what do you need to do? Think prayerfully about this. Then write down your answer in the space below or in a notebook.

Resolve to find out when the next prayer meeting is in your church, and then go. Put the date in your diary and make it a priority, if you possibly can. (If it's simply a matter of looking it up online or finding the information in a leaflet, try to do it now, before you forget!)

Now, before you spend a few minutes in intercession, choose three things to pray for:

1) Something in the world news.
2) Something in your nation – perhaps a leader or a situation.
3) Something local – in your community, church and family.

PRAYER: Thank Jesus that through his death and resurrection heaven's doors are open and we can approach God in confidence and love, and pray for all sorts of things. Thank Jesus that he is our Master and model, as he intercedes right now.

Ask the Holy Spirit to teach you to pray intercessory prayers. Then spend some time praying into each of the three areas named above. Have a Bible near and be listening for God's voice as you seek to see what the Father is doing and join in, through prayer.

Pray for your church to grow in intercession, and to see much fruit from this crucial and often undervalued aspect of prayer.

Further Reading:

Beni Johnson, *The Happy Intercessor* (Shippensburg, PA: Destiny Image, 2009).

$\boxed{\text{J}}$ is for Joyful

When we pray, there's a mindset that followers of Jesus are supposed to have. A demeanour we're encouraged to bring. An approach we're urged to adopt. It's the mindset that Paul says he has at the beginning of his letter to the Philippians as he prays for them: 'In all my prayers for all of you, I always pray with *joy*'.[1] Joy is the answer. Joy is the attitude. That's why **J is for Joyful**.

Jacquie is a friend of ours who's just returned to her home in Botswana after a number of years in the UK, having been part of our church and the small group that meets in our home. As we said goodbye to Jacquie, it was good to have an evening looking back on the time she spent with us and to thank God for her, before sending her on her way in prayer. One thing my wife, Sam, said that evening is that she'll always remember Jacquie's joyful prayers. I asked Sam more about this and she said: 'Jacquie prays with enthusiasm and passion. She prays thankful prayers. Believing prayers. But I've also noticed something about the way she prays for difficult situations. Instead of spending much time pouring out the problem before God, she names it and then spends most of the rest of her prayers recognizing and thanking God that he is more than capable of dealing with it. She thanks him for his power and love and sometimes mentions a story in the Bible where he changed a similar situation. To be able to pray like this,' Sam said, 'you need to know the Bible and know God.' And of course, Sam was right.

I've attended prayer meetings that are joyful. And prayer meetings that are not! Joyless prayer gatherings are hard work. They're life-draining and faith-sapping. You end up discouraged, dispirited and disheartened. That's not how it's supposed to be. Of course there are times when tragedy takes place and a community mourns (see **S is for Sad**) but, generally speaking, our prayers should be joyful because when we pray we fix our eyes on our Saviour Jesus, we remember who he is and what he's done and we ask him to bring his joyful and transformative kingdom of love. Also when we pray, the Holy Spirit comes, expanding our vision, bringing fresh hope and lifting our spirits. In short, when we pray, God brings joy.[2]

But it's even better to come to God in prayer *already* joyful and *already* expectant – knowing that God is good and longing for us to spend time with him and to hear our prayers. So how do we get this joy? Jesus tells us in John 15 and 16.

First, we can't manufacture joy, because true joy comes from knowing God. In fact, it comes from the heart of our joyful God. That's why Jesus calls it 'my joy' that he wants to be 'in' us.[3] Joy comes from living in relationship with God and is given by the Spirit as we rejoice that Jesus died and rose again for us.[4] As we know this joy deep within, it helps us live prayerful lives, walking in the Spirit.[5]

Second, to live joyfully and to pray joyful prayers does not mean we live in cloud-cuckoo-land, immune from the pain of the world or the many frustrations of life. What it means is that as Christ-followers we have a new story which we inhabit. A new mindset by which we live. A new heart which empowers us. This brings us a contentment that is not dependent on circumstances. It is what Jesus describes in John 16 when he says 'no one will be able to take away your joy'.[6] It is what Paul talks to the Philippians about at the end of his letter[7] when he says: 'I know what it is to be in need, and I know what it is to have plenty. I have learned the secret of being content in any and every situation, whether well fed or hungry, whether living in plenty or in want.'[8] This is joy.

To pray joyful prayers does not mean we live in cloud-cuckoo-land, immune from the pain of the world or the many frustrations of life.

We sometimes mix up joy with happiness. Happiness is great! We all love to be happy and want people around us to be happy. But happiness is an emotion and as such it is temporary, and rightly so. It's not right that we're happy when we encounter selfishness or injustice. But we can be joyful – all the time – because joy is not an emotion. It's a state of being. It's how followers of Jesus are supposed to be. It's how we're meant to pray.

Third, we get more joy as we pray and see God answering prayer. This is what Jesus means when he says: 'Ask and you will receive, and your joy will be complete.'[9] There is a link between hearing testimonies of answered prayer and experiencing greater joy. That's why it's good regularly to share stories of what we see God doing as we observe his kingdom changing lives and situations.

Sometimes, when I'm caught up in something difficult or I've watched some depressing news on TV, I find my joy waning. I've learned that at such times I have to look back and see where I let go of my joy and, as I pray and read the Bible, consciously choose to pick up joy again. That's not always easy. But I know the Holy Spirit wants to help me with this, so I normally ask him. And when I ask, he always reminds me of the contented joy I have in Christ and gives me more. At such times I wonder why I don't ask more often to live the joyful life! I know that Ann Voskamp is right: 'The brave who focus on all things good and all things beautiful and all things true, even in the small, who give thanks for it and discover joy even in the here and now, they are the change agents who bring fullest Light to all the world.'[10]

All this affects how we pray, and how we lead others in prayer. Of course we're not meant to whip up people into joy when we lead, but we are meant to help God's people pray joyfully, knowing that the Lord is good and that his kingdom knows no end. This is why I need God's help when leading anything, especially a prayer meeting. Leading others in prayer is about so much more than just coming with a list of things to pray for. I'm discovering that it's crucial to come with the right attitude so I can lead God's people in joyful prayers.

Lots of joyful prayers are described in the Bible. A great example is Miriam's prayer in Exodus 15, which she sang to God after the Lord had helped the Israelites cross the Red Sea and escape the pursuing Egyptian army. As she prayed we're told that she 'took a tambourine in her hand, and all the women followed her, with tambourines and dancing'.[11] The Psalms, which are our main biblical resource for praying, end in Psalm 150 by encouraging God's people to worship and pray using similar outward expressions of joy. Another biblical example is the joyful attitude Habakkuk had to life and prayer, even when things were difficult for him and for God's people. This is summarized so well in the conclusion of his prophetic book, where he says:

> Though the fig-tree does not bud and there are no grapes on the vines,
> though the olive crop fails and the fields produce no food,

though there are no sheep in the sheepfold and no cattle in the stalls,

yet I will rejoice in the LORD, I will be joyful in God my Saviour.[12]

Habakkuk shows us that joy provides an inner resilience and strength which empowers God's people. And he's right. It's why Nehemiah says to a people seeking to be prayerful and faithful in the midst of criticism, persecution and opposition, that 'the joy of the LORD is your strength'.[13]

So as disciples approach God in prayer, we come with joy. Even when life is difficult and when there are things going on that annoy us, or that we simply don't understand, we joyfully bring them to our joyful God. All this should affect not just our praying but our living. And it should inspire us to keep praying. More and more. Praying with joy.

ACTION: Spend some time resting in God's presence. Recognize the joy that he has put in your heart. Be thankful.

There are all sorts of things that come our way that can numb our joy, so much so that sometimes we can feel like we've lost it. If that's you, look back and see where you seem to have lost your joy and write a few notes about it in the space below or in your notebook. Then write how you would like to pick it up again.

PRAYER: Now turn all this into prayer. Thank Jesus that he is a joyful Saviour who loves to give us his joy. If you feel like you've lost your joy, talk to God about what seems to have caused it and ask him to restore it. Read Psalm 51:12. Ask for a fresh experience of his joy.

In particular, think of an example of an answered prayer – either in your own life or perhaps in someone you know or in your church. Give thanks and allow greater joy to stir within you.

Now let this joy infuse your prayers. Pray for yourself, your loved ones, your church and your community with joy.

End by asking the Lord to help you walk in the Spirit, bringing joy to your surroundings today. Pray that this would honour Christ and be helpful to those you spend your life with.

Further Reading:

Johannes Hartl, *Heart Fire* (Edinburgh: Muddy Pearl, 2018).

K is for Kenosis

In order to pray with love, attuned to the will of God, I need to come to God free of my own agenda. I need to lay down my ambitions and good ideas and instead seek the Lord for his desires and God ideas. I need to empty myself of 'me'. This is called self-emptying and is sometimes known as *kenosis*. That's why **K is for Kenosis**.

There's no better role model for kenosis than Jesus himself. Jesus chose to become the God-man: fully God yet fully human.[1] He left heaven and came to earth and was born as a human baby. He did this so he could serve humanity, becoming the long-prophesied suffering servant.[2] In doing this Jesus embodied kenosis, emptying himself and subjecting himself to human limitations. He knew what it was to enjoy food, but also what it feels like to be hungry. He worked hard and walked many miles and so got tired. He liked telling stories and jokes and no doubt enjoyed laughter, but he also wept when he was sad. He knew the love of family and human community, but at the end of his life he experienced betrayal, false accusation, torture and a horrific death by crucifixion. To do all this, he had to empty himself. The apostle Paul understood this and writes about Christ in Philippians 2, saying:

> He existed in the form of God, yet he gave no thought to seizing equality with God as his supreme prize. Instead he emptied himself of his outward glory by reducing himself to the form of a lowly

servant. He became human! He humbled himself and became vulnerable, choosing to be revealed as a man and was obedient.[3]

Kenosis is about humility. It's about going low. Getting your hands dirty. It's about becoming like Jesus and learning from his sacrificial life. It's about choosing to live by someone else's agenda. This is not about becoming a doormat and being pushed around and abused. Rather it's about knowing there's a higher purpose, a greater vision, and a more noble calling that we're to live by. It's kenosis that motivates us to get up early to pray (see **M is for Morning**), to intercede at times and places that seem inconvenient (see **I is for Intercession**) and to fast when many are feasting (see **F is for Fasting**).

Living like this – by another person's agenda – is described in the Bible as *meekness,* and is what Jesus meant when he said 'Blessed are the meek'.[4] As such meekness is a brave characteristic. To the unobservant, meek looks weak, but to those who have eyes to see, meek reveals strength. It's a wise and an excellent choice. That's because there's no better life than living God's way. Submitting to his word and walking in the Spirit is the exciting journey into the unknown terrain of discipleship that changes the world – and changes us – for good. There is much reward for this life – partly now and fully in eternity. That's why, when Jesus said 'Blessed are the meek' he went on to say 'for they will inherit the earth'. These challenging and perceptive words about meekness form part of what's called *The Beatitudes* – which describe a number of surprising attitudes and characteristics of disciples of God's kingdom. These attributes should not only shape our lives but inform our prayers.

Over the years I've seen examples of people living like this that arrest my attention. One such person is Karen, my sister-in-law.

She helps lead Beacon House of Prayer in Stoke-on-Trent with my brother William, and is a committed person of prayer. As well as praying at all times of day – and sometimes night – she gives time to listening, supporting and standing alongside people who are broken and have been through difficult times and find themselves in the prayer house. I know she'd say she sometimes gets tired and irritable, but if she does, it's rarely seen, as she obediently and faithfully serves her God and the people the Lord puts in front of her.

Heidi Baker, who works with some of the poorest people in the world, knows what it is to be faced with crowds of people in great need. Her answer is simply to love the one in front of you. I remember in 2011 reading *Compelled by Love*, which is Heidi's reflections on *The Beatitudes* of Jesus, and finding myself weeping as I read. The stories of kenosis – of love and sacrifice – and her understanding of the compassionate heart of Jesus, moved my heart again and again. Writing later with her husband, Rolland about kenosis, she says this:

> The biblical word kenosis describes what Jesus did. It is derived from the Greek word for 'emptiness' and describes the self-emptying of one's own will to become entirely receptive to God's divine will . . .
>
> Jesus emptied Himself and became nothing so He would be totally dependent on Holy Spirit, totally reliant on listening to His Father's instructions. Why did He do that? So you could follow Him.
>
> He didn't have to do it. He could have accomplished His mission another way. He could have shown up in gold robes and said, 'Listen to me! Do what I say!' But instead He chose to come as a baby, live among the poor, learn languages.

He did it for the sake of love, so we could imitate Him. So we too could walk in faith, pray for the sick in His glorious name and see them get up and run. So we could pray over a lunch and see it feed a multitude.

What kind of people does God fill? Empty ones.[5]

To pray with grace – with true love – and to be full of the Spirit of Jesus as we pray, we need to lay down our lives and empty ourselves of ourselves. As Mark Batterson says: 'the Holy Spirit can't fill you if you're full of yourself'.[6] This involves giving God all our sin and selfishness. It includes letting go of any bitterness or belligerence. It comprises of being honest about our desires to be cosy and comfortable. And instead we choose simply to follow Jesus. We go where he goes. We say what he says. We do what he does. We trust and obey. And in particular, we pray.

Obedience is highly underrated when it comes to prayer. When we know God is asking us to do something and we honour him with our obedience, then kingdom power is released. In the 1970s, John Wimber prayed for healing for many people, knowing from reading the Bible that the Lord was asking him to do this. None of the first 100 people he prayed for were healed. He felt like giving up, but he knew that the Lord was asking him to empty himself and give up looking good, and simply pray in obedience. Then one day, one person was healed. And then another. And that was the start of a significant healing ministry.

Mary, the mother of Jesus, is a lovely example of a life laid down in trust, obedience and prayer. That's probably why God called her to this role.[7] When, as a young unmarried girl, she was visited by the angel Gabriel and told that this was God's plan, she was naturally uncertain and concerned. But, once the angel had explained things, we see her exemplify kenosis as she lays down her own plans and agenda and says: 'I am the Lord's servant… May your word to me be fulfilled.'[8]

To live a meek, prayerful life like this is a good life. It's a humble life. In fact, prayer is one of the key signs of humility in a person. After all, prayerlessness signifies no need of God. Prayerfulness signifies dependence on God.

> Prayer is one of the key signs of humility in a person. After all, prayerlessness signifies no need of God.

Mother Teresa, the twentieth-century saint who worked with the poor in Calcutta, expressed it like this:

> Without a spirit of sacrifice, without a life of prayer, without an intimate attitude of penance, we would not be capable of carrying out our work.[9]

This life of prayer and sacrifice is the life Jesus modelled. As we come to pray like this, we ask the Lord what *he* would like us to pray for, more than just coming with our long lists.[10] We find ourselves praying for *others* more than ourselves. As we live and pray in this way, so we realize that our own material needs are relatively small – and that God promises to look after those things in any event when we seek first him and his kingdom.[11] What we need more are the eternal resources of 'faith, hope and love'[12] – resources the Lord loves to give to disciples who empty themselves of themselves.

ACTION: Take a few moments to pause and consider what issues this chapter raises for you. Write some notes either in the space below or in your notebook.

As you think about self-emptying – that is, emptying yourself of yourself – look into your heart and see if there is anything you need to let go of. A sinful habit you'd rather keep than lose. A grudge you hold because you just won't forgive. A desire for an easy, comfortable life that makes it hard to say to the Lord that you'll follow him wholeheartedly. Be honest with yourself – and name them before yourself and God. If it helps, write them down in the space below or in your notebook.

PRAYER: Now pray and give to the Lord anything you need to let go of. Empty it out of your life and hand it over to Jesus. Become empty.

The place of emptiness can feel like a vulnerable place, where so much is uncertain. Tell God that you trust him in that place, that he will lead you and take you into a good future.

Now ask him to fill your emptiness with the Holy Spirit. The Lord loves to answer this prayer. Keep asking him to fill you today, and that you'll continue to stay empty to your agenda, and rather be filled with his.

Finally, pray for someone you know who is serving God sacrificially in a difficult context. Give thanks for their life and service, and pray they'd continued to live the life of kenosis, loving the one in front of them today.

Further Reading:

Heidi Baker, *Compelled by Love* (Lake Mary, FL: Charisma House, 2008).

L is for Liturgy

Sometimes when we pray it's right to choose our words carefully and to use pre-prepared words before we pray. I do this especially when I've been asked to pray at a special event – like a wedding, or funeral, or celebratory occasion. Time might be short and I want to use my prayer-words well. At times like this I might use words, and sometimes a structure of prayer, that others have already used for similar occasions. In fact, there is a wealth of such material available. Prayers like this are called *liturgy*. That's why **L is for Liturgy**.

When Jesus gave the disciples *The Lord's Prayer*, he was giving them liturgy to pray. He was giving them words. Helpful words. Guiding words. Powerful words. Words to use. Regularly. The Bible is full of liturgy, as the prayers of many are recorded not just for interest's sake but so we can pray them too. So their words can become our words. Many of these prayers are found in the book of Psalms, which cover most eventualities of life. That's why many Bible-reading programmes include a psalm each day, encouraging Christ-followers not just to read them but to pray these psalms back to God. God has left them for us as his inspired word. We pray them back to him as inspired prayers.

> The Bible is full of liturgy, as the prayers of many are recorded not just for interest's sake but so we can pray them too.

Some of my favourite liturgical prayers in the Bible were written by Asaph. Asaph was one of the worship leaders and songwriters during the days of King David and he wrote Psalm 50 along with Psalms 73–83.[1] Psalm 73, for example begins with praise, acknowledging the goodness of God but soon gets brutally honest (see **H is for Honesty**), with Asaph telling God how he envies the godless who seem to be doing well. He pours out his heartfelt prayers to God, sharing his concerns. And then in verse 17, the tone changes. He enters God's presence and begins to truly worship. That affects everything and he's given new perspective. In response he tells the Lord in prayer:

> Yet I am always with you;
> you hold me by my right hand.
> You guide me with your counsel,
> and afterwards you will take me into glory.
> Whom have I in heaven but you?
> And earth has nothing I desire besides you.
> My flesh and heart may fail,
> but God is the strength of my heart
> and my portion for ever.

I have used this prayer of Asaph many times over the years, especially when I feel like I'm losing perspective. When I do that, I'm praying someone else's words. As I do so, these words of liturgy become my words. They help me to pray.

John Sentamu is the Archbishop of York. He's my Archbishop. He's the ninety-seventh occupant of that role and is a man of deep prayer. As well as seeking to be prayerful throughout the day, he awakens early to read the Scriptures and pray (see **M is for Morning**). Often his prayers are extemporary (see **E is for Extemporary**) – unscripted words from the heart – but I know he also loves to use pre-prepared liturgy in his prayers. He values the prayers of the saints.[2] Being an Archbishop in the Church of England, he is not only used to such prayers, but genuinely values the liturgy of the church. The Church of England regularly approves new liturgy, welcoming prayers that are both theologically orthodox[3] and helpful for particular occasions and prayer needs. Liturgy like this shapes us. It teaches us. It helps us to pray. It finds itself in prayerbooks and is a great resource for the life of prayer.

The *General Thanksgiving*, mentioned in **G is for Gratitude**, is a great example of a liturgical prayer, and can be found in the Church of England prayerbook called *The Book of Common Prayer*. But there are hundreds and thousands more liturgical prayers, found in all sorts of prayerbooks. You can buy them online or pick them up from a new or second-hand bookshop. I have friends who have a number of such books, and they dip into them at different times or perhaps during particular seasons in life or in the rhythm of the year – like during Advent[4] or Lent.[5] Some value the poetry of well-constructed phrases or the beauty of ancient words, reminding them that their faith is rooted in time and history. All this can be very helpful, providing words for us, especially when we struggle to find them for ourselves.

However we must take care not to over rely on liturgy. It's possible for me to use liturgy because I feel lazy and can't be bothered to find my own words. It's possible for me to say liturgical prayers while not really praying at all, as my heart isn't in them or maybe I'm actually thinking about something altogether different. It's possible for me to choose wonderful words from a prayerbook more for the charm of the words' sound, rather than the meaning and sentiment of the prayer itself. It's possible, when leading prayers in public, to choose words that

I hope will make me look good, rather than God. All this is unhelpful and wrong. Externally it might all seem and sound wonderful, but inside the thoughts, desire and motivations can be impure. So I need to take care. I don't want the words Jesus said about some of the religious leaders of his day to be said about me: '[They] honour me with their lips, but their hearts are far from me.'[6] To avoid all this, I must test my heart.

Sometimes when I pray publicly, I wonder whether I should use a pre-prepared liturgy or pray extemporary prayers. On more formal occasions, it's right that the words are all pre-prepared. There's nothing wrong with this. But there are many times when the answer of course is that it doesn't need to be either/or. I've learned that I can do both, even when I'm praying on my own. I can bring a liturgy which provides some structure as well as words, but then use this to insert my own extemporary prayers in various places. I can pause, giving space for silence and reflection. Liturgy can be used creatively. It can become a wonderful prayer gift.

One of the privileges of my role as a church leader is to pray with people at every stage of life. Sometimes I pray with followers of Jesus who are struggling with dementia. This is not easy as what they say is far from logical and often they make little or no sense. What I've learned is to assume that they understand everything I say and try to use liturgical words that they might have heard and used in the past. I might start with familiar Scripture, like 'The LORD is my shepherd' from Psalm 23:1. I will often pray *The Lord's Prayer* and maybe the blessing prayer of Numbers 6:24–26. What's fascinating is that they will often join in. It's like they come out of their confusion for a while and join me in prayer. I recall praying like this for my wife's elderly great-aunt who had quite well-advanced Alzheimer's disease, and as I began to pray *The Lord's Prayer* she stopped babbling and started to join me and as she did so, her eyes lit up and she began to smile. Then at the end of the prayer, after the 'Amen', she returned to her confused self. Moments like that are precious. They show us that many things, particularly liturgy, are remembered and get stored somewhere very deep in the human brain to assist us when praying.

Praying liturgical prayers on a regular basis can be so helpful. Their repetition gives us not only words to pray now but also helps us to memorise them for use at any time, in any situation, as needed. Don't underestimate their power, especially when prayed from the heart.

ACTION: Did you pray any liturgical prayers when you were younger (e.g. *The Lord's Prayer*, or some other prayers)? Which do you remember, and how much? You might like to try to write down in the space below or in your notebook a prayer you remember.

Are you surprised by what you recall?

Now think of the present. What liturgy do you use now, in your own prayers and at church? Take some time to think about this. You may use more than you think. Again, use the space below or your notebook.

PRAYER: Have a go at writing your own liturgical prayer today. Start by thinking about something you'd like to say to God (e.g. it could be adoration, it could be a request, for yourself or someone else). Then write your prayer – using the space below or your notebook. You might want to work on it a few times, to make sure the words say what you really mean.

End this prayer time in silence for a moment, and then pray your completed liturgical prayer to God.

Further Reading:

Northumbria Community, *Celtic Daily Prayer* (London: Collins, 2005).

$\boxed{\text{M}}$ is for Morning

We can pray any time, any place and anywhere, but there's no better time than first thing in the morning. That's why **M is for Morning**.

Once we understand that following Jesus is all about relationship rather than ritual, this not only gives new life to our prayers, but makes us want to pray. We long to talk with the One we love! We want to have daily conversations with God. And given that the Lord has been with us through the night (see **N is for Night**) and is with us as we awaken, it should become increasingly natural for our first thought to be God-directed, thanking him for the night and welcoming his presence in the new day. You can do this even before you step out of bed. Once you're up, it's good to set aside some special daily time to talk with God about the day ahead and the world he's placed us in. This puts God first – in his rightful place. To pray and read the Bible first thing makes so much sense.

As we read the Bible we discover that women and men of renown did just this – they gave time for prayer in the morning. The list includes Abraham,[1] Jacob,[2] Moses,[3] Joshua,[4] Hannah and Elkanah,[5] David,[6] the sons of Korah,[7] Job,[8] Daniel,[9] Anna[10] and many more, as well as the Lord Jesus himself, who 'very early in the morning, while it was still dark' often 'got up, left the house and went off to a solitary place, where he prayed.'[11]

The same is true if we scan church history. Augustine (354–430), Benedict (480–547), Anthony (1195–1231), Teresa of Ávila (1515–82), John Wesley (1703–91), the men and women of the Clapham Sect (c.1790–c.1830), Charles Simeon (1759–1836), George Müller (1805–98), Watchman Nee (1903–72), Mother Teresa (1910–97) and John Stott (1921–2011) are just some of those who chose to wake early to pray. There's something important about praying in the morning that all these people discovered.

I'm a morning person. When I wake up, my mind is usually active fairly quickly. I normally have my best ideas and my freshest thinking first thing. That's always been the case for me. In my naivety I assumed that would be the case for Sam, my wife, when we married. It took me a while to realize that she is not a morning person. Far from it. She finds it hard to engage in important conversation first thing and one day, when no doubt I was frustrating her with my early morning enthusiasm, she told me in no uncertain terms that I should cut talking so much over breakfast and wait until later to bring up important things. I was shocked, but her bluntness was actually what I needed to hear. Now I've learned to give her space in the mornings! Space to rise slowly. Space to come round. Space to be. And yet Sam still spends that first part of the day in Bible reading and prayer. This was harder when the children were young, especially the Bible-reading part, although she found that breastfeeding and praying seemed to work quite well together. But now our children are older and she has the option of having her focused prayer-time later when she's potentially sharper, why does she still prioritize the morning? The answer is she wants to talk with Jesus straight away, despite feeling sleepy. She wants to offer God the people on her heart, the day ahead and have him at the very centre of the day. She doesn't want these precious times of intimacy and intercession to be left for later. She's chosen, even though it's not easy, to prioritize the mornings. I love that decision and I think the Lord does too. Maybe that's why she's become such a woman of prayer.

Mary Kissell agrees. In her recent autobiography, church leader Mary describes a number of 'key moments that I look back on as being pivotal in shaping my faith . . . Most important', she says, '. . . was the decision to get up one hour earlier to learn to pray. A simple table in a Cornish kitchen proved to be a place of transformation.'[12]

Martin Luther, the sixteenth-century church reformer, prayed daily, particularly prioritizing the mornings. He said: 'If I were to neglect prayer but a single day, I should lose a great deal of the fire of faith.'[13] Luther also recognized that some people find it difficult to know what to pray, especially first thing, so he wrote down various prayers to help. Here's his Morning Prayer:

> I thank you, my Heavenly Father, through Jesus Christ, Your dear Son, that You have kept me this night from all harm and danger; and I pray that You would keep me this day also from sin and every evil, that all my doings and life may please You. For into Your hands I commend myself, my body and soul, and all things. Let Your holy angel be with me, that the evil foe may have no power over me. Amen.[14]

Beni Johnson believes there's something special about these early hours of the morning, especially when you pray with others. She may well be right when she says: 'We have learned through experience that, when praying at sunrise, there is an open Heaven. It feels like a straight shot right from Heaven to earth.'[15] Maybe that's why King David prayed first thing. In Psalm 5 we're given a glimpse of what he did:

> In the morning, LORD, you hear my voice;
> in the morning I lay my requests before you and wait expectantly.[16]

He learned to offer all his prayers to God first thing, and as he did so he then expected God to answer them. This is another good reason to pray first thing. It raises faith (see **B is for Belief**) and confidence that God is not only with us but will answer our prayers. It means we can come into all the situations we face envisioned and empowered, ready for all that lies ahead.

Another reason why it's good to prioritize prayer in the mornings is that mornings are such a great time of day! Watching the day awaken, seeing the sun rise and the first rays of light appear are a wonder to behold. Enjoying the silence and the unhurriedness of these early hours can be delightful. Those who make the time to get up early discover this. In his excellent book, *Morning*, Allan Jenkins includes a number of examples of people who rise early. These include Anna Koska, illustrator and beekeeper, who says this: 'It feels like a gift; it just took me a while to realise. There's a lightness of thought that feels untethered from the body, yet absolutely yanks at my soul to come fly.'[17] Celebrity chef Jamie Oliver likewise says that the early mornings are 'where time goes at normal speed instead of fast forward'.[18] Alex Soojung-Kim Pang in his book *Rest* has shown that 'Many notable creatives do their most intense work early in the morning, when their minds are freshest and least prone to distraction'.[19] So why wouldn't we want to use these creative early hours of the day to spend time in the presence of God, and pray?

Of course, to pray in the morning doesn't mean that we then neglect prayer during the rest of the day. The Bible teaches us that we should be prayerful throughout the day[20] (see **R is for Relentless**). We can also take a few moments – even a few minutes – at other times of day to focus on prayer, as Jesus often did,[21] and as Psalm 55 tells us: 'Evening, morning and noon, I cry out . . . and he hears my voice.'[22] This is all about fulfilling the call to be 'faithful in prayer'.[23] This faithfulness is not just about having a good prayer time once every week or so, but about keeping going – praying every day. When we do this we follow the example of King David who, in Psalm 145 says: 'Every day I will praise you . . .'[24] Those who've learned to get up early and pray every day know that it is of infinite value.

I have found this. Since the age of about 15 I've made time, first thing in the morning, to read the Bible and pray. That's part of my routine, every morning. At first I had to work hard, not only at waking up but also avoiding all sorts of morning distractions, but now, some thirty-five or so years later, it's much more of a habit. It's what I do. In fact, it's become the most important thing I do in all my day.

> I've made time, first thing in the morning, to read the Bible and pray. It's what I do. In fact, it's become the most important thing I do in all my day.

There may be reasons why some can't prioritize prayer in the morning. For example, you might work night shifts, or have young children who are demanding first thing. If that's you, don't worry that you can't pray early. Just do the best you can, and if or when circumstances change, then pray in the mornings. You won't regret it! Mark Batterson knows this, saying: 'I'm more and more convinced that the biggest difference between success and failure, both spiritually and in your future, is the wake-up time on your alarm clock. If you snooze, you lose. But if you pray through, God will come through as surely as the sun will rise.'[25]

ACTION: What is your present morning routine? Do you make time to read the Bible and pray? Write down either in the space below or in your notebook what you normally do.

If, having read this chapter, you would like to prioritize prayer more in the mornings, what would you need to do? Could you readjust your morning schedule? Or do you need to reset your alarm clock? Giving just fifteen minutes a day, at least to start with, will revolutionize your life. Write down what you intend to do.

PRAYER: Now turn this to prayer, thanking God that he is with you, and asking for his help particularly to pray in the mornings. If you're not used to this, thank the Holy Spirit that he gives self-discipline (see 2 Timothy 1:7) and ask him to help you cooperate with him in growing in this discipline, so it becomes a habit.

Now offer your day to God. Your time. Your energy. Your resources. Your thoughts. Your desires. Your friends and loved ones. Thank him that you are in a relationship with him, and pray that this relationship would grow, as you become increasingly faithful in prayer.

Further Reading:

Time to Pray: Prayer During the Day and Night Prayer from *Common Worship: Daily Prayer* (London: Church House Publishing, 2006).

$\boxed{\text{N}}$ is for Night

The longer I follow Jesus, the more convinced I am that prayer in the night is an important aspect of prayer that's rarely discussed. I don't mean praying before you sleep, although that's a really good thing to do (see **X is for eXamen**). I mean praying in the night – both when you're awake[1] but also when you're asleep. That's why this short book devotes a chapter to this. It's why **N is for Night**.

What happens to us when we sleep is still something of a mystery to scientists. Much research is still being done on this, and some fascinating literature is being written. What we definitely know is that sleep is very important to us.[2] Not only does it regenerate our bodies, giving us the physical rest we need, but something significant takes place in our brains. Christians have always believed that God the Creator is behind what is happening to us as we sleep; after all, God invented sleep. It was his idea. As we sleep so God is at work – not just in our bodies and brains, but deep in the human heart and spirit, ministering to us. Psalm 127 alludes to this when it says, in the alternative translation of verse 2, 'for while they sleep he provides for those he loves.' This means that God's people can know his presence, power and love whilst sleeping.

We don't know exactly how this works, but we see something of this both in the Bible and in the experience of Christ-followers. For example, there are many biblical characters who encountered God in the night through dreams, including Abraham,[3] Jacob,[4]

Job,[5] Joseph,[6] the wise men[7] and Pilate's wife.[8] Dreaming, which for most of us happens at night, is an important means of God communicating with us and according to the New Testament is a sign of God's new covenant and the presence of his Spirit with us.[9] Obviously not every night-time dream is a message from God, but sometimes a dream comes that arrests us and we need to take it seriously. Such dreams may be a form of prophecy (see **P is for Prophetic**) which Christ-followers need to learn to interpret wisely and well.

Jacob is a Bible character who had a number of night-time encounters with God, involving dreams, visions, words and angelic encounters.[10] The stories of his life show him to be a flawed and very fallible person, who often got things wrong. Despite his imperfections, God was with him and used him. This reminds us that experiencing God at night is not necessarily a sign of spiritual maturity. It also tells us that God wants to communicate with us, and that the night-time is often a good time to do so.

The Bible also describes God speaking in the night outside of dreams, to people such as Samuel,[11] Nathan,[12] Daniel,[13] Zechariah[14] and Paul.[15] Some of these were through 'visions', which probably happened as they awoke at night, and some through 'words' which again we assume God gave as they awoke from their sleep. Many followers of Jesus know what it is to wake in the night and pray. Sometimes this is for very practical reasons – because you're awake tending a baby, or ill, or maybe even going through a period of insomnia. Other times we awaken knowing that either the Lord wants to speak to us, or with a strong desire to pray (see **Y is for Yearning**). Madam Guyon, a faithful woman of prayer who lead the Quietist movement in France in the seventeenth century, would often wake in the night with such a sense of God's presence that all she could do was pray and worship.[16] When she prayed she would often intercede (see **I is for Intercession**), calling out to God for others.

In the 1960s when my father was a young ship's doctor on board a vessel crossing the vast expanse of the Indian Ocean, he developed a sore throat, so he put himself on antibiotics. In his autobiography he describes what happened next. The medicine

> seemed to have no effect. I looked at my pharynx in the mirror and saw what seemed to be a large abscess – a quinsy. My text books suggested that it should be incised. I dare not do it myself, and my assistant the Chief Steward did not have a steady hand.
>
> Back in Doncaster [in the UK], Jim Smith who was a member of Hexthorpe Methodist Church, was suddenly propelled out of his bed in the middle of the night. He started to pray for [me], but he didn't know why. Next morning, a Tuesday, he went into the Market and found my Father. 'Luther,' he said 'I was awoken in the night and told to pray for Richard. He is in some sort of trouble, but don't worry, it's going to be alright.'[17]

And my father was alright. Amazingly, the abscess began to heal and there was no need for surgery and all was well.

Sometimes God communicates with us at night in other ways. I've experienced his prophetic voice speaking to me as I come out of sleep, and sometimes even while I'm sleep. I know this has happened because I awake with a word already on my mind or a person to pray for. I know he's been speaking to me as I'm sleeping. Normally I've not been thinking about these situations or people before I sleep, so this gets my attention.

Occasionally I've gone to sleep asking the Lord about a situation and I then wake up with a clear sense of knowing what to do. Sometimes I go to sleep asking the Lord for help with a message I am to deliver the next day, and as I wake up I have one or a number of fresh thoughts to bring. It feels like these have been planted in my mind as I sleep. Maybe this is part of what the Song of Solomon means when it says: 'I slept but my heart was awake.'[18] Bill Johnson talks about this, saying, 'God loves to visit us in the night and give us instruction that we would have a harder time receiving during the day.'[19]

If the Spirit of God can speak to us in the night, which he sometimes does, it is not unreasonable to think that our spirit can pray to God as we sleep. That deep inner part of ourselves, awakened as we start following Jesus, can be praying to the Lord. This idea is stronger in the Catholic tradition of the church, which has often encouraged night vigils and recognizes that there is often a meeting between our spirit and God's Spirit at night. I know something of this for myself, because quite often I wake up in the night praying. It's not that I wake up and then start praying. I'm already praying. I'm already talking to God as I come out of sleep. Sometimes I'm worshipping him and other times I'm in conversation with him. There is clearly something of a mystery to this, but it reminds us that our relationship with God is not put on pause as we sleep. Once we start following Jesus, we enter a relationship for life that is truly 24/7.

> Our relationship with God is not put on pause as we sleep. Once we start following Jesus, we enter a relationship for life that is truly 24/7.

Kris Vallotton, one of the leaders of Bethel Church in Redding, California tells a story about this. A few years ago he was speaking at a conference and shared a twin-bedded room with Bill Johnson. On the first evening he went to use the bathroom in the night and had to pass by Bill's bed, so he crept quietly across the room hoping not to awaken him. As he neared Bill's bed, he was surprised because Bill was speaking, very quietly, under his breath, while asleep. As Kris listened, he could hear Bill's words. He was praying. He was saying words such as 'Jesus, I worship you. Jesus I love you'. Kris was moved by this, because this happened each night. Bill was asleep, yet praying. It's possible that King David was referring to something of this when he wrote in Psalm 63: 'On my bed I remember you; I think of you through the watches of the night. Because you are my help, I sing in the shadow of your wings.'[20]

Sam and I have a close friend called Liz Anson. Liz's mother is now a good age, in her late eighties. For many years Liz's mother has heard angels singing at night. Virtually every time she lies down to sleep she hears them. It brings her comfort and peace. Liz made us smile recently describing something her mum had said about them, saying: 'Sometimes they get quite loud which makes it difficult to sleep, so I have to tell them to be quiet!'

Some people dread the night. It's a time when they feel lonely or afraid. That is not what the Lord wants anyone to experience at night, as Proverbs 3:24 makes clear: 'When you lie down, you will not be afraid; when you lie down, your sleep will be sweet.' So ask the Lord for peaceful, healing, sweet sleep.

Some disciples have never experienced God at work at night-time, through a dream, a wake-up to pray or in any other form. If that's you, don't worry. That doesn't make you any less a follower of Jesus. Rather recognize that the Lord is definitely at work in you, whilst you are sleeping. The Bible is clear on this – saying 'even at night my heart instructs me'[21] – so give him thanks. If you would like to encounter God at night, then ask and be open and ready. You might like to keep a notebook by your bedside in expectation. I find that the more I ask, the more I experience, so much so that I now look forward to sleeping – not just because of the physical rest I'll get, but also because I know the Lord is going to be at work in me. All sorts of prayer will be going on, while I'm asleep at night. This makes the night-time exciting and opens up whole new possibilities in prayer.

ACTION: If this is an area of interest for you, read some of the Bible stories and look up some of the Bible references in this chapter. Be attentive to your thoughts and reflections. Use the space below or a notebook to record them.

Think about your experiences of God at night-time. Have you ever encountered God's presence or voice at night? If so, list some examples either in the space below or in your notebook.

PRAYER: Thank God that he is working on us and in us, while we sleep. Thank him for the night that's been and the day that lies ahead.

If you would like to encounter him more in the night, ask him. Then be expectant. And be ready.

End by praying for another follower of Jesus who you'd like God to watch over and be at work in whilst they sleep. Pray for an opportunity to talk to them about this in the future.

Further Reading:

Common Worship: Night Prayer (Compline) (London: Church House Publishing, 2014).

$\boxed{\text{O}}$ is for Opportunity

Followers of Jesus are called to change the world through prayer and action. As we pray, it's good to ask for God-given opportunities to be used by him. The Bible encourages us to pray like this. That's why **O is for Opportunity**.

> Followers of Jesus are called to change the world through prayer and action.

The picture of an open door is a metaphor used on a number of occasions in the Bible to illustrate the idea of asking God for opportunities. Paul uses it in Colossians 4, saying: 'Devote yourselves to prayer, being watchful and thankful. And pray for us, too, that God may open a door for our message . . .'[1] This simple illustration reminds us that God opens doors through prayer.

Sometimes these doors are literal doors. I remember as a young boy of about 7 finding myself stuck in the hotel bathroom of Kilravock Castle. We were on holiday, staying in this old stone castle in the Highlands of Scotland and I was three storeys up, having turned an old rusty key to lock the door that I then wasn't strong enough to unlock. I called for help. My brothers came but couldn't help. I began to cry, and my father came. He urged me to keep trying, but to no avail. We tried everything, including getting the key out and attempting to push it under the door for him to turn from the other side, but it got stuck halfway through, so I pulled it back and returned it to the lock. It just wouldn't unlock. My crying turned to sobbing as I imagined myself locked in the old castle bathroom forever! Then my father told me to stop. To stop turning the key. To stop and wait, because he wanted to pray. I recall him praying a simple prayer, asking the Lord to unlock the door. I said a tearful 'Amen' from the other side, and then he said, 'Now try again.' I did – and the key immediately turned smoothly in the lock and it clicked open, and out I came. I was so happy! This experience was significant for me, because it left me with a deep appreciation of the power of prayer. From that moment I knew that prayer changed things. I knew that God opens doors through prayer.

> God opens doors through prayer.

In the early days of the first church, Peter experienced this too in Jerusalem. In Acts 12 we're told that James, the brother of John, was arrested and killed. Then Peter was also arrested and he and the church were concerned for his future. One night, when 'Peter was sleeping between two soldiers, bound with two chains, and sentries stood guard at the entrance', God sent an angel who rescued him as everyone was asleep, causing the chains to fall from his wrists, allowing him to pass by the guards without being noticed. Eventually they came 'to the iron gate leading to the city. It opened for them by itself' and we're told 'they went through it'.[2] Peter was free. He just walked through and out. From there he went to the house of Mary the mother of John, which was full of people praying for him. The door was answered by a young girl who was so surprised to see him that she went to tell the people inside while still leaving him outside, banging on the door! Those gathered didn't believe at first it was him and so for a while he was left knocking at the door, until it was eventually opened and he was let in. This is a story all about God opening doors through prayer – particularly the doors of the prison. Peter's persistent knocking is also a prophetic picture of the importance of persistent prayer (see **R is for Relentless**) as well as a telling reminder to Christ-followers that the answer to our prayers is sometimes right in front of us – just the other side of a door opened through prayer.

When we pray for an open door, we're asking the Lord to make a way. To open up an opportunity. David Watson, who was the renowned and respected vicar of St Michael le Belfrey in the 1970s and early 1980s was a gifted evangelist. One reason why he was so effective was that he asked the Lord, every day, for an opportunity to lead someone to faith in Christ. He asked the Lord to open a door. And the more he asked, the more the door opened. And the more the door opened, the more expectant he was, ready to seize the moment. I have found this when praying for all sorts of things. For example, when I'm about to pray for someone, or I'm entering a home, or I'm visiting a church to speak, I often ask the Lord for a prophetic word to share, and invariably the Lord gives me something helpful. It feels like a door of opportunity is opened through prayer.

God opens doors of opportunity for all sorts of things, especially for evangelism – for proclaiming the good news of Jesus. Acts 14:27 describes this, with Paul and Barnabas telling the church in Antioch 'all that God had done through them and how he had opened a door of faith to the Gentiles'.[3] 1 Corinthians 16 similarly refers to 'a great door for effective work' that had been opened for evangelism in the city of Ephesus.[4] And in 2 Corinthians 2:12 Paul describes going to Troas 'to preach the gospel of Christ' and finding 'that the Lord had opened a door'. These doors are normally unlocked through God answering the prayers of praying disciples.

My friend Paul Myers has found this in his life. Paul is an evangelist. He loves telling people about Jesus and is gifted in communicating the gospel – the good news of Jesus – in such a way that people often respond. Paul has a powerful story of what God has done in his life, freeing him from a life of addiction and fear[5] and, like David Watson did, he now prays regularly for evangelistic opportunities. He especially prays for this before he and the team he leads goes out onto the streets, or before he speaks at meetings. He knows that opportunities come as we pray.

Some of these doors of opportunity provide access not only into the lives of individuals, but also to families, streets, communities, other people groups and even nations (see Acts 14:27). Only Christ can open these doors, but as co-labourers with him and members of his body, part of our prayer assignment is to intercede and take our stand against spiritual powers that keep doors shut. Those who have served in pioneering mission contexts know that prayer is foundational to their work. As we cry out to God on our knees in intercession, Christ can open the door to a city, region and nation.

When we pray for doors to open to large groups of people, we're praying for revival. Renewal is when the Spirit of God is poured out on the church. Revival is when the Spirit overflows and impacts beyond the church, bringing many to faith and, in time, transforming society. Revival starts with prayer. As he scans church history, the Archbishop of Canterbury Justin Welby concludes that prayer brings renewal to the church and fresh hope to culture. That's why he says, in Pete Greig's *Dirty Glory*, 'there has never been . . . a revival in the church that did not begin with a renewal of prayer.'[6]

Jesus himself taught about doors opening through prayer, telling his followers on a number of occasions that they should 'knock and the door will be opened'.[7] Jesus knew that persistent knocking on the door of heaven through prayer has an impact here on earth. It really does open doors of opportunity!

It's easy to forget, however, that the door of opportunity still needs to be walked through. It's good to pray – which creates the opportunity – but it's possible then to miss the opportunity that God brings. We can pray and then fail to take advantage of what is put right before us. That's why prayer and action always go together. That's why we pray for brave hearts and courageous wills, so that we then embody our prayers. No one models this better for us than the One we follow – Jesus Christ himself.

ACTION: God presents all sorts of opportunities before us all the time, but as we've seen, he especially loves to do this in response to our prayers.

So can you think of a time recently when you asked the Lord to open a door of opportunity for something? When was it? And what did you ask? What happened? Take some time to consider this, and use the space below or in your notebook to write about it. (If you can't think of a time when you prayed like this, take some time to reflect on why not. Is it because you didn't know you could? Or because it never crossed your mind? Or something else? You might like to use the space below to make notes.)

Now think about a door of opportunity that you would like the Lord to open. Write it down in the space below or in your notebook, so you can see it before you.

PRAYER: Now begin to pray that the Lord would open this door, and do it soon.

Find a creative way to do this. So you might like to draw a picture of an open door in the space below or in your notebook. Or you might like to go to the door in the room you're in and start knocking on it (or otherwise knock on a nearby table, or chair leg, etc.) as an act of prophetic symbolism. You might find this really helps you to pray, especially as you come back and pray again and again and again. Have a go!

Further Reading:

E.F. and L. Harvey, *Kneeling We Triumph, Book One* (Richmond, KY: Harvey Christian Publishers, 2012 edition). Kindle edition.
E.F. and L. Harvey, *Kneeling We Triumph, Book Two* (Richmond, KY: Harvey Christian Publishers, 2012 edition). Kindle edition.

P is for Prophetic

If prayer is conversation with God, then when we pray we should expect not just *us* to speak to God, but for God to speak to us. This shouldn't surprise us, given that the Bible describes Jesus as 'the Word' of God.[1] Various names have been given for hearing God's voice in this way, including *prophecy* or *the prophetic*. That's why **P is for Prophetic**.

Jesus told his disciples that he was their 'good shepherd'.[2] He compared them to sheep who needed leading. It's a simple and very effective illustration that still applies to disciples today. We need a shepherd and his name is Jesus. Jesus also said 'My sheep listen to my voice',[3] reminding us not only that Jesus wants to speak to us, but also that we're created with the capacity to hear the voice of Christ.[4] To believe and practise this is not a sign of mental instability! Quite the opposite. It points to the close relationship God desires to have with all his children. Tania Harris writes about this in *God Conversations,* saying:

> We need a shepherd and his name is Jesus.

> Perhaps you've heard a voice but you haven't seen a face. You sense a force, but you haven't met a person.
>
> The voice is not your own, it's not your intuition or your thoughts, it's not a wave of abstract forces in the universe. It's the voice of a person who longs to be heard; the God who wants to be known.

The voice is not only heard by those who ticked the boxes of religiosity or live the life of the super-spiritual. It's not a voice that's confined to those born in the Bible belt or those who've been schooled in theology. It's a voice that reveals a God of relationship, the God whose essence is love – who reaches out to us wherever we are. A voice that comes to those who are listening.[5]

Whether we realize it or not, we start following Jesus in response to his voice. The Lord calls us, and we respond. Some know this for sure – they are certain that Jesus has spoken to them. Others think it's their choice, but then as they look back they begin to realize that the Lord had been calling them all along.[6] Having been called by him, he wants the relationship to grow as we spend time in his presence and prayerfully allow his word and Spirit to guide and shape us. It's all part of the adventure of discipleship!

The story of the call of Saul[7] is a fascinating example of a God encounter in the Bible involving the voice of God. It's first recorded in Acts 9. When Jesus speaks to Saul, Saul hears the voice but doesn't know who he is. That's why Saul says: 'Who are you, Lord?' and the One behind the voice says 'I am Jesus'.[8] Caught up in the same story is a man called Ananias, who later goes to pray with Saul[9] in response to the voice of Jesus. Ananias has been following Jesus for a while, although we don't know for how long. He's not a church leader or mentioned elsewhere in the Bible as someone of renown; he's simply described as 'a disciple'[10] – a Christ-follower. His response to the voice of the Good Shepherd is notably different to Saul's. Here's what Acts says:

The Lord called to [Ananias] in a vision, 'Ananias!'
'Yes, Lord,' he answered.[11]

118

So whereas Saul asked who he was, Ananias didn't. Ananias simply said 'Yes, Lord' because Ananias knew the One speaking to him. He knew the voice of Jesus. That's the Lord's desire for all disciples.

> Ananias knew the One speaking to him. He knew the voice of Jesus. That's the Lord's desire for all disciples.

The Lord speaks to us today in a number of ways.[12] The main way is as we read the Bible because the Bible is 'the word of the Lord'. That's why it's good to put prayer and Bible reading together. Whenever I read the Bible, I ask the Lord to speak. And he does.

'How do you discern the voice of God?' asks Mark Batterson. Here's his answer. 'It starts with the Word of God' – the Bible. 'If you want to get a word *from* God, get into the Word of God.'[13] That's good advice!

Basically, the whole of the Bible is God's word,[14] and as we read it God speaks and we are changed. His message sinks into our minds and hearts, and helps us to think and live differently.[15] This work of God's Spirit takes time – in fact it takes a lifetime. It's a slow but good work. However, there are times when we read the Bible and the message just jumps off the page. It feels like the Lord is particularly speaking with a word in season. A word for now. A word I especially need to hear. The written word becomes a prophetic word.

Sometimes this happens not just when we're directly reading the Bible, but when we're focused on the Lord in prayer or worship, sometimes though a dream, vision, picture or word that comes to us. This often happens to me when I'm praying with someone. The Lord gives me a prophetic message to share to encourage them. Prophecy should do this, with Paul reminding the Corinthians that 'the one who prophesies speaks to people for their strengthening, encouraging and comfort'.[16] It can also happen, as it did to Saul, as we're going about our day and God's voice just breaks in. When we hear his voice in this way we need to listen and obey. That's because God's word is transformative and always brings life.

Most disciples find it takes time to learn to hear the voice of God. As our relationship with Christ grows, so we get to know him and his voice more clearly. I've also learned, unsurprisingly, that sin numbs the voice of God. That's why it's good to be quick to say sorry (see **C is for Confession**).

> Sin numbs the voice of God. That's why it's good to be quick to say sorry.

When you come to pray, don't worry if you don't hear the prophetic voice of God every time. Some people do, but many don't. Just talk with God anyway, and be open and attentive to him speaking. Read the Bible, and be listening for his voice. Talk with him. Ask him things. Have a notebook to record how you sense he's guiding you. It can be good to have a more mature disciple or mentor or spiritual director to talk with about this. If your heart is open, and you want to hear, the Lord will begin to attune your ear to his voice. In fact, he wants to. He wants his disciples to hear his prophetic voice more and more, which is why the Bible says 'eagerly desire gifts of the Spirit, especially prophecy'.[17]

As we're attentive to his prophetic voice, so the Lord will guide our praying. We will feel a nudge or desire to pray in a certain way. When we intercede (see **I is for Intercession**), it's good to see if the Lord gives us insight to direct us. We might feel it important to speak blessing prayers over people or a community. These kinds of prayers can be particularly prophetic, as we declare good things like healing, joy, freedom, forgiveness, reconciliation, provision or protection over people. When we pray like this, we use words like 'May' or 'Let', perhaps picking up phrases from some of the Psalms of blessing in the Bible.[18] The Ffald-y-Brenin community in Wales have, in recent years, used and modelled this kind of blessing prayer helpfully and effectively and there's much we can learn from them.[19]

Often when we start praying, something or someone comes to mind, and so we trust that the Lord is planting these thoughts in us in order than we might pray. Sometimes when he does this he gives us a particular message that we sense isn't just for our prayers, but is meant to be shared. This sometimes happens to me, and when it does I always ask who it's for, and if I have permission to share it. Whenever I'm given a prophetic message it always needs to be prayed over. In my experience, many Christ-followers fail to do this. Perhaps they're in a meeting or with someone and the Lord speaks to them about a situation or person and they share it rather too quickly. Discernment is needed. I encourage people to go through a simple three-step process of discernment.

First, *revelation*. This is about the message itself. The scripture, word, picture, dream or vision. It's being clear about the content of what's been communicated. It involves asking the question: 'Lord, what is the message?'

Second, *interpretation*. This is the meaning. The message could mean all sorts of things. So you need to pray, asking, 'Lord, what does this message mean?'

Third, *application*. This is about what you should do with it. You should be asking things like, 'Lord, is this for me, or someone else? If someone else, should I share it or not? And if so, when? And how?'

So discernment is needed. Discernment as we pray. Discernment if the message is to be shared. If the prophetic message is particularly significant and/or seems to suggest a change in direction for you or others, you should expect the Spirit of Jesus to confirm this (usually a number of times) and often through other people. It's good to write these things down and record them, whether prophecies come through you, or are given to you. I normally do this in my journal. I also have a prophecy wallet where I keep on cards prophetic words that have been given me over the years. I often reread these, sometimes taking them away with me when I travel, to remind me of the prophetic messages that have been spoken over my life.

No prophetic message should contradict Scripture and the Bible says it should be tested.[20] Sometimes this testing is done in community, especially if the word is shared in a church prayer meeting. That's what happened in the church in Antioch in Acts 13:

> While they were worshipping the Lord and fasting, the Holy Spirit said, 'Set apart for me Barnabas and Saul for the work to which I have called them.' So after they had fasted and prayed, they placed their hands on them and sent them off.[21]

I'd love to know more details about how the Holy Spirit communicated. In what form? And through whom? But we're not told. But we *are* told that the Spirit of Jesus spoke. That's what's important. And that the church then took it seriously and spent more time praying and fasting, no doubt as part of testing and discerning the message. As a result they sent out Barnabas and Saul on their first missionary journey, which resulted in many converts and new churches being planted.

It all came out of prayer. Prayer that became prophetic prayer.

ACTION: Can you think of a time, perhaps recently, when you prayed and it felt like the Lord guided you to pray in a particular way? Write it down either in the space below or in your notebook.

Now think of the last time you sensed the Lord speaking prophetically to you. Where were you? What happened? What did he say? What did you do with it? Did you go through the three-step discernment process? Record it below or in your notebook.

PRAYER: Ask the Lord if there is anything he would like you to pray about today. Be attentive to what comes to mind.

Now start praying about this, seeking to be led by the Holy Spirit as you pray. Is there anything the Lord wants to say about this situation? Do you sense he wants you to pray in a particular way?

Ask the Lord to help you today to intentionally 'walk by the Spirit', being open to his voice and guided by him. Pray this is the case wherever you go today.

End by praying that you will more and more 'eagerly desire gifts of the Spirit, especially prophecy' (1 Corinthians 14:1). Tell the Lord this is your desire and commit yourself to grow in this.

Further Reading:

Joyce Huggett, *Listening to God* (London: Hodder & Stoughton, 1986, 2016).

Q is for Quiet

Communication experts helpfully tell us that not all communication is verbal. Body language, posture, eye contact, appearance, touch and many other things also communicate strongly. In fact, many messages that we consciously or unconsciously send to each other are non-verbal. It's the same in prayer – communication with God. Sometimes the deepest and most meaningful times of prayer involve silence. Little or nothing is said. It happens when we're quiet. That's why **Q is for Quiet**.

This chapter on quiet prayer is not about what some call 'praying in your head'. That kind of prayer is good – using prayer-words formed in the mind but just not saying them out loud. For example, I might give God adoration, or confess or intercede, but do so without making any noise. An example of someone doing this in the Bible is Hannah, whose 'lips were moving but her voice was not heard'.[1] You might do that while sitting on a bus or going for a walk, especially if you don't want others to hear you. The downside of that kind of prayer is that it's very easy to wander off-track, which is why I often encourage people to speak their prayers out loud, if they can. Nevertheless, many pray like this and God receives it like all other kinds of prayers.

So if this chapter is not about *that* kind of silent prayer, what's it about? It's about consciously coming before God, but not speaking. It's about being silent in his presence. It's about what some call centring prayer,[2] allowing our very presence with him, and he with us, to communicate. Whereas devotional prayer is about actively listening to Jesus, being attentive to his presence and often conversing with him using words (see **D is for Devotional**), quiet prayer involves no words and is, literally, about being silent in his presence.

Whether we realize it or not, we do this in loving human relationships all the time. When a couple kiss, they're not saying anything, but they're communicating all sorts of messages to each other. When a mother holds her infant child. When a father hugs his teenage son. When a family member takes the hand of their aged relative. When we smile. When we wave. All these and more are examples of intentional communication without words. We can do the same in prayer, with God.

Psalm 46 is a prayer-song that recognizes and acknowledges God's presence, with the chorus: 'The LORD Almighty is with us; the God of Jacob is our fortress.'[3] It also includes the well-known words: 'Be still, and know that I am God . . . '[4] It urges God's people, in response to God's presence, to slow down and stop. Literally to be still before God and focus on him. Of course, this might involve using words. But it doesn't have to. Many have found they've encountered God and communicated with him at such times *without* using words. Those who've followed the example of St Ignatius use this kind of quiet prayer. It sometimes begins with words – perhaps with reading a Bible story a number of times and imagining yourself in the story as one of the characters. From this place of contemplation you then rest in quiet. Instead of speaking your prayer, *you* become your prayer. Ignatius said this about quiet prayer: 'It is better to keep silence and to be, than to talk and not to be.'[5]

> In quiet prayer, instead of speaking your prayer, you become your prayer.

This kind of praying takes intentionality. In our noisy world, where so many people plug in headphones whenever they have an opportunity for quiet, praying in this way only works if we choose silence. 'Silence', says Wayne Oates, 'is not native to my world. Silence, more than likely, is a stranger to your world, too. If you and I ever have silence in our noisy hearts, we are going to have to grow it . . . You *can* nurture silence in your noisy heart if you value it, cherish it, and are eager to nourish it.'[6]

This kind of praying also takes time. I normally can't do it in a hurry. If I rush, I find I can't focus and my mind just races off in all sorts of directions. And it's normally done on my own to avoid disturbance. To stop yourself getting distracted, you might find it helpful to have a notebook nearby. That way if you don't want to speak to God about the things that come to mind immediately, you can make a note of them and then pick them up later, without having forgotten about them. (You can also scribble down anything else that comes to mind – like something you need to do today, or something to add to the shopping list!) Once you've written down things that can now wait, you can settle and give yourself time and space to be in God's presence. Samuel Chadwick expressed it like this:

> The soul needs its silent spaces. It is in them that we learn to pray. There, alone, shut in with God, our Lord bids us pray to our Father which is in secret, and seeth in secret. There is no test like solitude . . . It would revolutionise the lives of most men if they were shut in with God in some secret place for half an hour a day.[7]

When I think of someone praying like this, I think of Hannah Bath, who's one of the staff at The Belfrey. Hannah works as our production manager, but when she's not helping us with technical things she loves to be in our House of Prayer. She's a woman of prayer, who loves God's presence. When she prays she often doesn't say very much. She knows that she doesn't need to. She values resting in God's presence. Enjoying his love. Encountering his Spirit. In the quiet.

People who pray this way sometimes find all sorts of creative means to express their prayers. Perhaps they draw. Or paint. They might make or construct something. It's for the Lord. It's a prayer. Of course, you might talk to God whilst doing this, which would be fine. But you might not. Just the very act of creating might be your prayer. It's conscious. It's intentional. It's quiet.

Lots of people in the Bible rested in God's presence in this way. Many of the prophets, such as Micah,[8] spent hours 'waiting on the Lord' which probably involved much time in quiet and contemplation. The writer of Lamentations knew something of this when he wrote: 'The LORD is good to those whose hope is in him, to the one who seeks him; it is good to wait quietly . . .'[9] I suspect that the apostle John also spent much time in quiet prayer. From first meeting Jesus, he had the closest relationship to him of all the disciples.[10] Church tradition tells us that he was the only one of the original twelve disciples who wasn't martyred and so went on to live a long life, and as he did so he became increasingly contemplative. His sermons often involved few words. He enjoyed being in the presence of the Lord. This is reflected in his three letters at the end of the New Testament, which have a strong emphasis on relationships – on living in love, abiding in truth, living in joy and being kind. It's this same John who on the island of Patmos had the profound God encounter that we now find in the book of Revelation, which includes experiencing 'silence in heaven for about half an hour'.[11]

It's fascinating that many who aren't followers of Jesus are today finding great value in silence[12] and some are discovering that there are all sorts of ancient resources to use it well, many of which come from followers of Jesus. Blaise Pascal, the great seventeenth-century philosopher and scientific pioneer, was a man of deep faith and Christian prayer who came to appreciate silence, saying: 'The sole cause of man's unhappiness is that he does not know how to stay quietly in his room.'[13]

When we give time and space for silence, we not only uncover ourselves to ourselves, we also disclose ourselves before God. Many find such vulnerability difficult, but when we break through the uncomfortableness of silence, we can find a place of wonder and joy in God's presence. This is a place where few words need be spoken. It's a place where we discover the value of quiet prayer.

> When we break through the uncomfortableness of silence, we can find a place of wonder and joy in God's presence.

ACTION: What stands out for you about this chapter? Write down your thoughts and reflections in the space below or in your notebook.

If you're going to put this kind of quiet prayer into practice, you need to make space for it. If you've never tried quiet prayer before, you need to find at least ten or more minutes to make a start. If you can, try to find that immediately. If you can't, go through your diary now and schedule in time to do this in the next couple of days. The PRAYER section below will guide you through praying in this way.

PRAYER: Now you've given yourself at least ten minutes for Quiet Prayers, settle yourself into a comfortable space where you can relax without falling asleep. Have a notebook at hand to record anything you want to pray about (or need to do) later. Now settle down and rest in God's presence. If it helps, start with a word of Scripture, like 'Be still, and know that I am God' (Psalm 46:10). From that you might like to speak a few prayer-words, perhaps some simple words of adoration, telling the Lord how much you appreciate him. But when you can, stop articulating your prayers in word form and be OK with not using words. Feel the silence. Practise being quiet. Recognize the Lord's presence. And rest.

At the end of this time of Quiet Prayer, you might want to register what it was like. What did you sense? What was good? What did you find difficult? Be honest. Tell the Lord that you value him and his presence.

If you want to grow in this form of prayer, ask him to help you. He will. But you too will need to give time and space. The more you do this, the more benefit you will see from this kind of Quiet Prayer.

Further Reading:

Ruth Haley Barton, *Invitation to Silence and Solitude* (Downers Grove, IL: IVP, 2004, 2011).

$\boxed{\text{R}}$ is for Relentless

Sometimes disciples of Jesus give up praying too easily. Don't do that, because there are many times when we must keep praying. We need either to keep going there and then, or come back another time and pray more. There is great value in persisting in prayer like this – praying relentlessly. That's why **R is for Relentless**.

Some people think you only need to pray once, and that's enough. After all, when Jesus taught on prayer, he told his disciples they should 'not keep on babbling like pagans'.[1] Surely God has heard the prayer, and so you needn't prayer any more? Such a view of prayer, though, is rather mechanistic. As we've been discovering, prayer is relational – it's a conversation with God. In human conversation, while sometimes we speak about something once and as a result everything is agreed and happens, very often we actually talk about the same thing a number of times before resolution. There's nothing wrong with this. In fact, it's a good and healthy thing and often means we end up with the issue working out much better due to the extended conversation. So it is in prayer. Some prayers take time. They need much more than one prayer. Actually, sometimes what's needed is many prayers over a prolonged period of time.

Epaphras is a Bible character who prayed like this, so much so that the apostle Paul described him to the church in Colossae as 'a servant of Jesus Christ' who 'is always wrestling in prayer for you'.[2] Paul intentionally uses physical, athletic language here to show that Epaphras knew the benefit of constant, regular prayer that was often hard work. John Eldredge is right when he says: 'Effective prayer is often like the felling of a great tree – it takes repeated blows.'[3]

Jesus knew this, which is why he told the story of the persistent widow, who pursued an unjust judge again and again until he gave her the reasonable thing she asked for. Jesus' point is not that God is like an unjust judge. Rather, it's that if an unjust judge will grant a persistent widow her good request, how much more will our good Father want to answer our prayers if we keep going? Luke makes this patently clear in his recording of the story, introducing it by saying: 'Then Jesus told his disciples a parable to show them that they should always pray and not give up.'[4]

Always pray and not give up. That's what persistent, relentless prayer is all about.

In another similar story about prayer, Jesus describes a hypothetical situation where you go to a friend in the middle of the night and ask for bread because your house guest has just arrived late.[5] This would be virtually unheard of in Jewish culture. You just don't do this. Instead you wait until the morning. But, Jesus says, you do it anyway, perhaps because the neighbour is your friend. Your friend is reluctant to get up and disturb his family, but eventually he does it. He helps you. Why? Jesus says it's 'because of your shameless audacity'.[6] You don't mind defying social convention. You ask your friend. This, says Jesus, is how God is with us when we come before him in prayer. He responds to our cheeky prayers! Especially the ones which are persistent, because Jesus then goes on to say that we should pray persistently. That we should

God responds to our cheeky prayers!

knock – and keep on knocking. And we should seek – and keep on seeking.[7] We mustn't be afraid to pray relentless prayers.

My brother William is someone who knows the value of relentless prayers. As he leads Beacon House of Prayer in Stoke-on-Trent, along with Karen and the team, he knows that many things only come after prolonged prayer. That's why over the past fifteen years he's devoted hundreds and hundreds of hours to prayer and intercession for all sorts of people and situations, especially for his city of Stoke and for the UK. He knows, as we've seen, that persistent prayer helps develop our relationship with God. He identifies with Bill Johnson, who says: 'Quick answers are fun, for sure, but delayed answers increase one's interest in the matter that is being prayed over. Delayed answers also shape the character of those who are to receive them. It could be said that *faith brings answers, but enduring faith brings answers with character.*'[8] William has learned that our prayers don't always get answered immediately. In fact, those involved in the House of Prayer and 24/7 Prayer movements all know this. They know they've signed up for the long haul. They know that while it's an honour to pray and that we come to pray with joy (see **J is for Joyful**), nevertheless praying persistent prayers is not always exhilarating and you need stamina and steadfastness, patience and much encouragement to keep going and press on.

As well as developing our relationship with God, there are other reasons why we need to keep going in prayer too. They include: for us to get to know the mind of Christ in a matter, because the Lord honours faithfulness and because of time delay associated with spiritual warfare (see **W is for Warfare**). Sometimes we don't get an immediate answer to prayer, but we just know that we need to persist. We're not really sure why, but we know we need to keep going. I often find this, and it reminds me that there is a mystery to prayer. I don't know everything about it or how it works. But I still know that God calls me to pray and that God loves to answer – especially my persistent, relentless prayers.

I've prayed for many people for healing over the years. I can think of countless examples where the prayer took just a few minutes and God answered instantly. But there are many times when one prayer wasn't enough and we needed to press on for longer – as well as lots of others when there seemed to be no progress (see **U is for Unanswered**). We've learned that our job is to pray; God's job is to heal. However, we're also discovering that sometimes we must give more time to pray – to pray relentlessly. Just recently I spent over an hour praying for someone for a particular healing issue, taking time to pray, to listen to the Spirit, to wait and then to pray some more. Often when praying for healing we will anoint with oil, as we're told to in James 5:14[9] and as a sign of welcoming the Holy Spirit. Sometimes we will come back again. Sam and I pray regularly for a woman in our church who has multiple sclerosis. There's no medical cure for her condition so we've committed ourselves to keep praying relentlessly for her. We've been visiting her every month now for about three years, to pray for her healing. Despite little progress to date, she still wants us to come, and we still want to pray. We're learning about persistent, relentless prayer.

It's said that the nineteenth-century evangelist D.L. Moody had a prayer list of 100 friends whom he wanted to become followers of Jesus. He prayed for them all regularly until, one by one, they gave their lives to Christ. By the time of his death, all but four were committed Christ-followers. The last four attended his funeral where the good news of Jesus was proclaimed. And on that day the final four all became followers of Jesus. Such is the value of relentless prayer.

We've already seen that it's good to pray every day – in the mornings in particular (see **M is for Morning**) and be prayerful throughout the day, as we recognize the Lord's presence with us. Being dedicated to prayer in this way is of great value. We're not to boast about this, but be humble about it,[10] which means not everyone needs to know about it, although the Lord will know. Occasionally others might see signs of our persistence and dedication in prayer, as they did with the writer of the letter of James, who Eugene Peterson tells us 'carried the nickname "Old Camel Knees" because of thick calluses built up on his knees from many years of determined prayer'.[11] I've known people like this, including my New Testament tutor at Wycliffe Hall in Oxford in the 1990s. He was a brilliant scholar with a humble, prayerful heart, who often had worn patches on the knees of his trousers – the product of much kneeling in relentless prayer.

Job is a biblical character who stayed faithful in his praying, despite difficult and discouraging circumstances. Jeremiah is another. He faced criticism, opposition and even physical violence, but kept on faithfully praying and delivering God's message.[12] The New Testament tells us that such perseverance is a fruit of the Holy Spirit[13] and something to be cherished. Social science research tells us that persistence is a hugely underrated and important character trait that's of great value.[14] In the history of the church, revival normally is precipitated not by a few occasional prayer requests for a fresh outpouring of the Holy Spirit, but by the relentless prayers of the faithful who keep on praying again and again and again.

I've been praying for the north of England, for renewal in the church and revival in society, for many years now. While I see some fresh shoots of new life in the church, the renewal I'm asking for has still not fully come, and certainly revival is not here. That's why I'm still praying. And I will continue. Relentlessly. Because nothing of lasting significance happens without prayer.

Pete Greig, the pioneer of the 24/7 Prayer movement knows this, which is why he speaks and writes with a passion on the importance of humble, relentless prayer. It's this kind of prayer that makes a difference. It's this kind of prayer that sees breakthrough. I know Pete is right when he says: 'The rusty hinge of human history turns out to be the bended knee.'[15]

> Humble, relentless prayer is the kind of prayer that makes a difference. It's this kind of prayer that sees breakthrough.

ACTION: When was the last time you saw benefit from persevering at something in life (maybe something at work, or in the family, or something more personal)? Write about it in the space below or in your notebook.

Now apply this to prayer. Begin by reading the story of the persistent widow (in Luke 18:1–8), asking the Lord to encourage you. Then think about the last time you relentlessly prayed with persistence about something or someone. What happened? Did you see fruit from your labour? Write about it in the space below or in a notebook.

PRAYER: As you come to pray, first ask the Holy Spirit to give you and grow in you the fruit of perseverance. Take some time over this, thanking him that he wants this for you even more than you do!

Now take a person or situation which needs persistent prayer. Name them (or it) before God and begin to pour out your heart to the Lord about it. Ask for his guidance to know how to pray, and keep praying. Ask him to keep giving you creative ways to pray, to keep it fresh and to help you keep going.

Further Reading:

Pete Greig and David Blackwell, *The 24/7 Prayer Manual* (Eastbourne: David C. Cook, 2010).

$\boxed{\text{S}}$ is for Sad

Even though our default setting for prayer should be set at joy
(see **J is for Joyful**), there are times when we come to God full
of sorrow and grief. Our hearts are not cheerful, but cheerless.
At such times it's right that we pray prayers of sadness. That's
why **S is for Sad**.

When we're sad we mustn't hold this back from God. We
need to tell him about it, in prayer. When we pray or sing in
this way, we're praying what's called prayers of *lament*. God
doesn't mind this, in fact he welcomes it. It's one reason why
the Bible includes quite a number of sad prayers and why God
has given over a whole book in the Bible to the subject, and
called it Lamentations. Even the book of Psalms, where the
main focus is on praise and thanksgiving, includes many songs
that are either partly or fully laments. Lament, says Pete Greig,
is 'a vitally important, often forgotten, expression of prayer'.[1]

My brother William and I recently took my elderly mother
to northern Italy to visit the grave of her older brother, Gordon.
He'd been killed there whilst serving in the British Army
towards the end of the Second World War. My mother, now
in her eighties, had never visited the grave and we knew she
wanted to do so before she died, so we were pleased to go with
her. The grave was in a beautifully kept Commonwealth War
Graves Commission graveyard, set on a hillside amongst olive
trees with nicely tended lawns surrounding row after row of
graves. We found Gordon's grave and read the inscription on

the gravestone giving his name, rank, number, date of death and age. Below that was a large cross and finally, towards the base there was space for the family to write a short message. His parents – my grandparents – had chosen these words: 'The LORD gave, and the LORD hath taken away: blessed be the name of the LORD.' Those words from the book of Job[2] were my grandparents' sad prayer – their lament. After all these years I felt their grief.

We spent quite some time at the grave talking about Gordon and also praying, giving thanks for his life and for his sacrifice. We then took some time looking at some of the other graves, particularly reading the messages that other families had written about their loved ones. On grave after grave were words from parents, widows and children, attempting to express in a short space both gratitude for the life lived and the sadness of their loss. It was a deeply moving experience, made all the more poignant because one of these men was my uncle, and that my mother – even though a young girl at the time of his death – was still able to recall the heartache in the family when the news of Gordon's death was received. She described the pain and anguish in her home. I got a sense of this being repeated again and again in family after family across our nation. Such loss. Such sadness.

The words of Job that my grandparents picked are well-chosen words for people of faith, although sometimes they're misinterpreted. The story of Job describes a man who goes through

> Sometimes all we can say is that we're sad. God understands.

much hardship, including the loss of all his family in tragic circumstances. How will he react? What will this do to his faith? Job's story is of a man who, rather than blaming

God, trusts God, even though Job is confused and grieving. Knowing Job's story gives context to the words on Gordon's grave, showing they don't mean 'life has been lost, praise the Lord!' What they mean is something much deeper and more trusting. They mean something like this: 'Lord, you gave us this person – the gift of this life. And now you've allowed this gift to be taken away. We don't understand why and we're sad and we mourn. But in the midst of all this, we trust you. We will even give thanks for their precious life and for many good things in life, recognizing your presence and our constant need of you. So even though it's hard, we trust you. And we even praise you, for we know you're always good.'

Sometimes when we're grieving it's hard to pray like this and to tell God that we trust him. Sometimes all we can say is that we're sad. We see that in the Psalms when we read words such as:

Listen to my cry,
for I am in desperate need . . . [3]

God understands all this. He knows it is often very hard. Indeed, Jesus himself said, 'In this world you will have trouble.'[4] But in time, and as we go through the process of grief, it's good to get to a place of trust. We see this in Psalms 42 and 43 where the psalmist says to himself:

Why, my soul, are you downcast?
Why so disturbed within me?
Put your hope in God,
for I will yet praise him,
my Saviour and my God.[5]

All this reminds us that God hears and receives our sad prayers and that they shouldn't be withheld from him. Rather, we need to pray from the heart (see **H is for Honesty**). As Johannes Hartl says: 'In prayer, God is not interested in pious theatricals; he's after our hearts. Wholly.'[6]

Often we find it difficult to articulate in prayer exactly how we feel, especially when we're grieving or mourning. That's why many find inspiration in using other people's prewritten prayers, such as those found in Scripture or in various liturgies (see **L is for Liturgy**). Psalms such as 3; 6; 12; 13; 28; 51; 56; 60; 77; 142 and others too, express deep emotions such as sadness and sorrow, frustration and fear, and even regret and remorse. The language used can often be strong and impassioned. God does not mind us praying like this. He's big enough to cope with it.

On my Uncle Gordon's grave is a cross. The cross is the simplest and best-known sign of the Christian faith. It points to heaven. It shows how Jesus' death on the cross opened the gate of heaven. Christ's death shouts that death and sadness is not the end. For all who trust in Christ, there's life and joy the other side of the grave, won by Jesus. But the cross is not just about heaven, for it also speaks of earth. The cross is made from a tree grown out of the earth and is rooted in the ground – in the complexities and pain of the world. And on this cross hung Jesus, suffering and in agony, which is often our experience here on earth. The two posts of the cross express this profoundly, with the vertical post reminding us that our prayers must be grounded in the realities of life, while the horizontal beam speaks of Jesus, who died with arms outstretched for every sin and sadness of life.[7] That's why it's good to cling to the cross in prayer.

I have by my bed a cross, given to me as a gift a few years ago. It's called a holding cross, and is beautifully crafted so as to fit snuggly in your hand, to especially grab and hold onto in the hard times. Sometimes I take hold of this cross when I pray, and particularly when I'm sad. It reminds me of the source of my strength and where hope can be found: in the cross of Jesus Christ.

Nearly thirty-five years ago, one of my predecessors as vicar of St Michael le Belfrey, David Watson, died from cancer at the age of 50. David wrote a number of excellent books during his life, the final of which he wrote while ill. In fact, it was about his illness and about pain, suffering and sadness. It was published after his death and called *Fear No Evil*. Writing it probably helped David process what he was going through. *Fear No Evil* is a gift to followers of Jesus, having helped many work through their own pain, grief, illness and mortality. Still read today, the book helps people lament. It recognizes that this side of heaven we do not experience God's kingdom in its fullness. We live in a world of sin, sickness and suffering. And while we do everything we can to work and pray for God's kingdom to come here on earth, we will only enjoy the totality of God's kingdom in heaven. And that will be a great and glorious day! But until that day, we pray and we trust. Even when it's so, so hard, we pray and we trust. We cling to the cross, discovering that there is strength for each day and more than enough hope for tomorrow.

The last words of *Fear No Evil* are about trusting God, and seeking him in prayer. These words have inspired and brought hope to many:

Whatever else is happening in me physically, God is working deeply in my life. His challenge to me can be summed up in three words: 'Seek my face.' I am now clinging to life (though I still believe that God can heal and wants to heal); but I am clinging to the Lord. I am ready to go and be with Christ for ever. That would be literally heaven. But I'm equally ready to stay, if that is what God wants.

'Father, not my will but yours be done.' In that position of security I have experienced once again his perfect love, a love that casts out fear.[8]

ACTION: When was the last time you were genuinely sad? What was it like? How did it affect you? Did you pray and tell God about it? Where did you find resources to help you? Write about it in the space below or in your notebook.

What stands out for you from this chapter, as you think about lament – praying sad prayers? Is the Holy Spirit asking you to do anything in response? If so, write it down either in the space below or in your notebook.

PRAYER: Are you sad about anything right now? If so, start to tell the Lord. Begin to pour out your heart to him, expressing your lament. If it helps, choose a psalm – like Psalm 6 – and find words that express your emotions and turn them into prayer. End, if you can, by telling God that you trust him in the midst of what you're going through.

End your prayers by praying for someone known to you who is struggling. Pray for them and for their circumstances. It's OK to pray for change. It's even more important to pray for them and how they are. If you can, send them a message of encouragement today, telling them that you appreciate them and that you've been praying for them.

Further Reading:

David Watson, *Fear No Evil* (London: Hodder & Stoughton, 1984).

$\boxed{\text{T}}$ is for Tongues

Many people find they don't always have the right words of appreciation to share with those they love. I find this. Sometimes I run out of words to tell my wife how great she is. Or the words I have just seem inadequate. Despite trying to be creative and using various means to express love, I sometimes wish I had a whole new language to do so. What's wonderful about the relationship that followers of Jesus have with God, is that there *is* just such a language of love that we can use, given by the Holy Spirit, to express praise and adoration to our Father. It's called *tongues*. That's why **T is for Tongues**.

> There is a language of love that we can use, given by the Holy Spirit, to express praise and adoration to our Father. It's called *tongues*.

Tongues, or as it's sometimes called, the *gift of tongues*, is a God-given unlearned prayer language. It's a supernatural gift of the Spirit,[1] which means it's not earned or deserved. It's just given. For someone who's never spoken in tongues, it can seem like a strange practice of prayer – something maybe for mature or particularly spiritual kinds of people. But the opposite is actually the case. Tongues is not a gift for the mature or a badge of spirituality, because in the Bible it's normally given towards the start of following Jesus as people experience the presence and power of the Holy Spirit. We see this on quite a number of occasions in Acts, as we read the story of the first Christians. For example, in Acts 10 the first Gentile (non-Jewish) believers were seen to be 'speaking in tongues and praising God' when they came to faith while Peter was preaching.[2] Also in Acts 19 we're told that in Ephesus 'Paul placed his hands on the [new believers], . . . and they spoke in tongues and prophesied'.[3]

Throughout most of church history there are examples of followers of Jesus who've prayed in tongues. In the fourth century Pachomius, who founded the first monastery, was said to be able to speak in both Latin and Greek despite never having learned them! The early Waldensians in the twelfth century, Vincent Ferrer in the fourteenth century, Francis Xavier in the sixteenth century, some of the Methodists in the eighteenth century, the Pentecostals in the twentieth century and many others are reported to have been able to speak in unlearned God-given languages.[4] It's a much more common form of prayer language for Christ-followers than many realize.

I didn't speak in tongues when I first became a believer, but I did a little later as I actively pursued a deeper relationship with God through the Holy Spirit. I asked some people to pray for me and as a result began praying a few words, but I wasn't sure if it was tongues or not. Then the following week, as I entered a church building a few minutes late and walked into an atmosphere of praise, I found that unlearned foreign words came freely flowing out of my mouth. I now pray in tongues regularly, in fact most days at some point. It's part and parcel of my ongoing daily relationship with the Lord. Sam's experience was different. She first spoke in tongues not as a result of anyone praying for her, but more spontaneously when riding her bicycle. She'd just become a Christ-follower and was quietly singing a praise song as she pedalled along, and then suddenly noticed she was using foreign words that she'd never learned!

When we speak in tongues, the Bible says that we're praising God[5] in prayer.[6] It's *to* God and *for* God and a form of adoration (see **A is for Adoration**). We see this particularly when this gift is given for the first time in Acts 2 where the believers are described as 'declaring the wonders of God'.[7] However, rather than coming from the mind – which involves thinking about and processing words – it comes from deep within – from our spirit.[8] We don't need to think about the actual words formed, rather they flow, like a song from the heart, in a prayer of love to God.[9] Like most forms of prayer, its main use is in private – to help develop our relationship with God in prayer.[10] When we pray to God in this way it very often builds us up in our faith, even if we don't understand in our minds what we've prayed. We know that God hears and receives it, with the by-product being that we're encouraged.[11] It can be a lovely thing when followers of Jesus pray or sing in tongues together, having a similar corporate effect of building us up together.

Occasionally the gift is used in public prayer, when someone prays out loud in tongues for all to hear. The Bible is clear that this should only happen when the speaker is prompted by the Spirit to do so, and the church should then wait for the interpretation to come,[12] so there's some understanding of the prayer of praise that's just been offered. It's significant that the Bible calls this an 'interpretation' rather than a translation.[13] The one who interprets is giving the sense of what is being said, not necessarily a word-for-word translation. So public use of tongues requires an interpretation. What should be avoided is lots of people one after another speaking in tongues with no interpretation which no one understands. That would be unruly and unhelpful.

When we pray in tongues we're using a language we don't know. The Bible says this could be a human or angelic tongue.[14] If it's a human language – no doubt spoken by some people-group somewhere on our planet[15] – then it is unusual, but just possible, that it might be understood by someone present. If that's the case, then the Holy Spirit has set that up as a means of getting their attention. That's what happened in Acts 2, with people from different countries saying that 'each of us hears them in our native language',[16] and it can occasionally happen today as people recognize someone speaking their language. However tongues more normally is not understood in this way, and doesn't need to be if it's used in private prayer. If spoken publicly, then an interpretation should helpfully be given. Occasionally the Spirit might prompt you to interpret your own tongue in private. I've done that on a few occasions, asking the Lord to show me what I've been praying, and I've then written down what I sense is the interpretation of my tongue.

You don't have to speak in tongues to be a follower of Jesus.[17] Down the ages many wise and godly people have never had or used this prayer language. It's not the main sign of being full of the Holy Spirit, as there are occasions in the Bible when people begin following Jesus and are immersed in the Spirit, but tongues is not mentioned.[18] If there is a gift or a sign of being Spirit-filled – that all should seek – the Bible says that is prophecy (see **P is for Prophetic**). However, this doesn't mean that tongues is not important or useful. It's a wonderful gift, one which Paul says to the somewhat tongue-obsessed church of Corinth he uses 'more than all of you'.[19] In fact, Paul says it's a gift he wishes all believers used.[20] That means that while not all believers *will* speak in tongues, or *need to* speak in tongues, they *can* speak in tongues. After all, it would be unkind and

152

inconsistent with the biblical understanding of a good God for him to urge people to use a gift that's not available to them! That's why I encourage people, if they want to, to ask for, and use this gift.

Sometimes I hear people say that because gifts of the Spirit are *given*, you shouldn't ask for them; instead you should just wait for God to give whatever he wants, whenever he wants. While that sounds noble, it actually shows a misunderstanding of our relationship with God. When it comes to God we come as little children,[21] to a Heavenly Father who is generous and lavish in his love and, as Jesus says, loves to give gifts to those who ask.[22] In fact, there's a sense in much of the Bible that he's longing for us to ask him.[23] So if you don't speak in tongues, ask the Spirit to release this gift in you. Sometimes it helps having someone else pray for you, perhaps gently laying hands on you.[24] Most importantly, seek the Holy Spirit more than this gift. He will guide you and help you. All the gifts of the Spirit belong to him, and he longs to give them away. That's why, when it comes to gifts of the Holy Spirit like tongues, the Scriptures urge us to 'eagerly desire' such things.[25]

In the history of the church, tongues is a gift that has sometimes been misunderstood and at times abused, particularly by those who've used it to show off their spirituality. To do that is not only immature, but unbiblical. In many ways, it's the least important of the gifts of the Holy Spirit, because it's mainly for personal use, whereas other gifts are better because they're normally used for the benefit of others.[26] However, tongues is nevertheless really helpful in building up the disciple, as well as often being a gateway to other gifts. As Bill Johnson says, 'one of the first gifts the Spirit gives to believers to release [new] things is the ability to pray in tongues because He knows we need this tool to train our hearts, minds, and bodies to perceive and agree with what He's doing'.[27] That's why tongues should not be despised or disregarded, but rather encouraged and used in prayer.

There are other benefits of tongues that are not listed in the Bible which Christ-followers have discovered over the years. Rather like fasting, it can be a means of releasing God's power into situations. Often I find that I pray in tongues when I don't know how to pray for a situation, and this seems helpful. Jackie Pullinger, who pioneered an extraordinary work of the Spirit amongst drug addicts in Hong Kong beginning in the 1960s, found tongues to be the most effective form of prayer to use when sitting alongside those going through addiction withdrawal. She urges followers of Jesus to use this gift for fifteen minutes each day. Many who've done that have found it to be a source not only of personal encouragement, but often the way into a whole new realm of powerful prayer.

So tongues is a powerful, lovely and valuable form of humble prayer. When we praise and pray in this way, let's not forget, as Guy Chevreau helpfully reminds us: 'Tongues are not a sign of high spirituality but God's resource for human inability.'[28]

ACTION: What has stood out for you in this chapter? Is there anything you need to do in response? Write it down either in the space below or in your notebook.

Ask yourself if you 'eagerly desire' gifts of the Spirit (1 Corinthians 14:1), like prophecy and tongues. If not, why not?

PRAYER: If you don't yet use the prayer language of tongues, why not ask the Holy Spirit to give you this gift? Having asked him, then start to use it. Just start speaking out one or two syllables or words. This can get the initial awkwardness out of the way, and then as you repeat it, the language often grows and flows. Don't forget you're starting to learn to speak a new language, so sometimes it's not easy at first! (If you're finding it hard to get started, it can be helpful to ask another follower of Jesus who uses this gift, to pray with you. Sometimes it's good to persevere too.)

If you do have the prayer language of tongues, use it now. Also, if you can, intentionally use it during the day today – perhaps when you're walking somewhere, or driving the car, or on a bus. As well as using it as part of your daily prayers, you can use tongues as a means of being prayerful throughout the day.

Further Reading:

Jackie Pullinger, *Chasing the Dragon* (London: Hodder & Stoughton, revised edn. 2006).

$\boxed{\text{U}}$ is for Unanswered

It's wonderful when we pray and God answers our prayers. But what happens when he doesn't? Why is that? Did the Lord not hear? Or did I pray incorrectly? Or from the wrong motives? The Bible says that God hears every prayer, and that he answers. But, to be totally honest, it doesn't always feel like that. That's why **U is for Unanswered**.

Unanswered prayer is an oxymoron – that is, an apparent contradiction. At least, that's what most followers of Jesus think. That's because the Bible says there's no such thing as unanswered prayer. As we've been learning in this A–Z, God loves to hear our prayers and always answers. He always does something. He always responds in some way.[1] As David says in the Psalms:

I call on you, my God, for you will answer me . . . [2]

And yet elsewhere in the same book of Psalms, David also cries out to God in frustration, saying:

How long, LORD? Will you forget me for ever? How long will you hide your face from me? . . . Look on me, and answer, LORD my God.[3]

So, how do we understand this dilemma? The answer is that God hears and answers our prayers, but not always in the way we ask. Why might this be?

There are lots of reasons why our prayers do not get answered in the way we ask. Here are five.

1. Sometimes what we're asking for is not God's will.[4] It may seem like a good idea to us, but the Lord has other plans. Better plans.[5] Plans that we don't see. That means we can pray and pray and pray, but because he's good, he will not answer in the way we ask. Many Christ-followers can think of times when they've asked the Lord for something and the answer hasn't come, and now, looking back, they're grateful that he didn't answer as they'd originally asked. As C.S. Lewis said, 'If God had granted all the silly prayers I've made in my life, where would I be now?'[6]

2. Sometimes it's not the right time.[7] God is a master time-keeper and, as the saying goes, the Lord has perfect timing: he's never too late and never too early. He knows when is best. Sometimes I am impatient, and want the answer right now. On many occasions, especially early in our marriage, Sam and I had unexpected bills – for example, on the car – that we just didn't have the money for. So we prayed. And on every occasion, the money came in, sometimes in extraordinary ways, but often on the very last day! God's timing was perfect, but at the same time he was teaching us about patience and trust.

3. Sometimes we don't ask with the right motivation. We might think we do at the time, but if we were really to examine our hearts, we'd see that our inner attitude isn't right. For example, we might be praying from a selfish motive. Or asking for a way out of a situation that we need to take responsibility for. The Lord sees all this, knowing our hearts and our motivations. The writer of James specifically names

wrong motivations as a reason for unanswered prayer, saying: 'When you ask, you do not receive, because you ask with wrong motives . . .'[8] In particular, if we are deliberately sinning and not wanting to put something right with God, that especially numbs us to his will and creates a blockage to our prayers.[9] When we don't forgive others our hearts become embittered and there's no means of true reconciliation. Many fail to realize this also influences the effectiveness of our prayers.[10] When we forgive those who have wronged us, it doesn't excuse sinful actions, but it does mean we don't harbour bitterness towards them. Forgiving others changes our hearts and empowers our prayers.

> Forgiving others changes our hearts and empowers our prayers.

4. Sometimes there's much more spiritual warfare taking place than we realize[11] (see **W is for Warfare**). We normally don't see this, as it takes place in the unseen heavenly realm, which means that we can get frustrated at what seems like a lack of an answer. But it may be that there's something going on behind the scenes that either delays the answer or influences things so that the answer doesn't come when or in the way we ask.

5. And sometimes we just don't know. We don't know why our prayer hasn't been answered. This has been my experience on many occasions. I've sought the will of God. I've acknowledged that his timing might not be the same as mine, knowing that his timing is always perfect, and yet it feels late. I've tested my heart and confessed all my sin. I've put on the armour of God and I've fasted and prayed persistently and relentlessly. And my prayer has not been answered. Why? My conclusion is that I probably will never know. So I need to trust.

Trust is very important when it comes to prayer, particularly when my prayers seem unanswered. Trust is part of having faith, believing that God understands and will always work for the best[12] (see **B is for Belief**). Trust is at the heart of all relationships, especially our relationship with God. That's why it's good to pray and not give up (see **R is for Relentless**). Also, prayer is not like a computer programme where certain inputs produce a predictable outcome. That's far too cold and mechanical. No, prayer is relational. It's intimate conversation with the Lord, who is love. This relationship can cope with uncertainty and some things that are unknown. In fact, this side of heaven there will be much that is unknown. In eternity we will, as the Bible says, 'know fully'.[13] We'll be able to ask the Lord about any and every supposed unanswered prayer, and we'll then understand why. But for now we trust. And we need to trust, because our relationship with God, despite being one of love and friendship, is not an equal relationship. We can't know and understand everything, like he does. He is God, and we're not. He is all powerful, and we're not. He knows best, and we don't.[14] And so we need to trust him. Deeply trust him.

The apostle Paul is a character from the Bible used greatly by God and who saw countless prayers answered. But he also wrote in 2 Corinthians 12 about a prayer that God left seemingly unanswered. He called it 'a thorn in my flesh' as it was obviously difficult and painful for him. 'Three times', he says 'I pleaded with the Lord to take it away from me. But he said to me, "My grace is sufficient for you, for my power is made perfect in weakness."'[15] Theologians down the centuries have pondered what this 'thorn' might be. In the end, we don't know. And it's probably good that we don't know, because not knowing allows us helpfully to apply this not to just one particular kind of unanswered prayer, but to many. It reminds us that some things in life are really hard. And some prayers just don't seem to get answered. And yet God is still good and still a prayer-answering God. And his grace – his unconditional, undeserved, and unending love – is more than enough.

> Some prayers just don't seem to get answered. And yet God is still good and still a prayer-answering God.

Founder of the 24/7 Prayer movement, Pete Greig is a follower of Jesus who knows all about this. He's seen some amazing answers to prayer in his life, but also knows about the need to trust God when his prayers for his wife to get better didn't get answered as he expected. His bestselling book on this, called *God on Mute: Engaging the Silence of Unanswered Prayer* has helped many. In the book Pete is frank and honest (see **H is for Honesty**) about his struggles with prayer, urging us to keep praying and recognizing that there is a mystery to prayer. He so helpfully reminds us that God never asks us to cover up for what might seem, to us, to be his mistakes![16]

When God seems not to answer prayer, he actually knows exactly what he's doing. So don't let that stop you praying. Instead, keep going. And keep trusting. As Mark Batterson says, 'If you can trust God when the answer is no, you're likely to give Him praise when the answer is yes. You need to press in and press on. By definition, praying hard is praying when it's hard to pray.'[17]

ACTION: Look again at the five main reasons (among many) why prayer may not be answered. Think about a prayer you've prayed which God doesn't seem to have answered. What did you pray? Why did you pray this prayer? Looking back now, do any of these five help explain why it might not have been answered? (You might like to use the space below or your notebook to record your reflections.)

Look at your heart. Has it become hard or cynical about prayer, as a result of a seemingly unanswered prayer? Is there anything you need to do, in order for your heart to become soft and open, and to pray again in faith, trusting that God really does hear and will always answer for the best?

PRAYER: Now turn these thoughts to prayer, asking for the guidance of the Holy Spirit as you offer them to God.

In particular, revisit the seemingly unanswered prayer, noted above. Tell the Lord about your frustration and disappointment with the outcome. Ask him to show you his perspective on it. Ask for his help to trust him with the outcome.

Close by praying that your relationship with the Lord would grow strong and closer, whatever the outcome of your prayers. Thank him that he is totally trustworthy. Pray that you'd discover that more and more today and in these coming days.

Further Reading:

Pete Greig, *God on Mute: Engaging the Silence of Unanswered Prayer* (Eastbourne: Kingsway, 2007).

$\boxed{\text{V}}$ is for Vision

Many people pray for small things. Detailed things. Like the difficult meeting coming up at work later today. Or a family member who's ill with a particular virus. Or the missionary family just arrived overseas who've asked for prayer to learn the language and get to know locals. All those things are important and certainly worthy of prayer. But we're also called to pray for more substantial matters. For churches, city councils and governments. For towns, cities, regions and nations.[1] For a fresh outpouring of Holy Spirit faith, hope and love. For cultural renewal. For social transformation. To pray like this we need vision – the ability to see the big picture. That's why **V is for Vision**.

There are plenty of examples through history of people who've prayed like this. These include people such as William Wilberforce, the social reformer behind the abolition of the slave trade, and Mother Teresa of Calcutta, founder of Missionaries of Charity, who prayed and worked for poverty to be relieved simply by going to the poorest people she could find, in India, and serving them. In York where I live, I think of Barrie Stephenson, who for many years has been praying to see homelessness ended in our city, and also worked to see this become reality through starting the charity Restore and through other excellent social action projects.

The Bible is full of encouragements to pray visionary-type prayers. Paul tells the new believers in Ephesus that their God is 'able to do immeasurably more than all we ask or imagine, according to his power that is at work in us'.[2] I suspect Paul could imagine God doing much, and yet he describes God as being able to do much more than that! This is a call to pray big, bold prayers. To the God of immeasurably more.

Praying like this requires vision. Vision that comes from the Bible and is inspired by the Spirit. Vision is a picture of the future that produces passion. It's having the capacity to see a new day. A new destiny. A new trajectory.

> Vision is a picture of the future that produces passion. It's having the capacity to see a new day. A new destiny. A new trajectory.

God gave Abraham such a vision, when he told him to go out and count the stars and then said that his descendants would outnumber them![3] To respond to such a vision required prayer, trust and faith (see **B is for Belief**), which is why Abraham is called 'the father' of faith.[4] God gave Esther such a vision when, despite the future looking bleak for her people, God told her, through her relative, that she was in a strategic position 'for such a time as this'.[5] God gave Nehemiah such a vision to rebuild the walls of his city, even though he wasn't an architect or builder. He committed the vision back to God in prayer[6] and as a result his vision inspired God's people to do in fifty-two days what hadn't been done for 140 years! God gave Anna, a prayer warrior who was committed to 24/7 prayer and worship, a vision for 'the redemption of Jerusalem'.[7] When she was very old, God allowed her to meet the infant Jesus when his parents brought him to the temple, and she knew the vision she had been praying for was to be fulfilled.

God still gives this kind of vision to people today. For particular people-groups – like women or men, or children, or people from certain social or ethnic backgrounds. For areas of injustice – exposing issues that need changing, like human trafficking, poverty, or various environmental issues. For personal and corporate transformation – perhaps through removing barriers to growth, or changing mindsets or hearts. Most importantly, the Lord gives vision for people to come to know him, and he wants his followers to be praying that for all sorts of people.

Esther Swaffield-Bray works for International Justice Mission – the largest international anti-slavery organization in the world.[8] God has given her a vision to see human trafficking ended, which she is pursuing through prayer and through her work. To hear her speak and to see her pray is an inspiration. There are times when her prayers are very specific, praying for detailed things, but she's also not afraid to pray big visionary prayers, asking for governments and nations to change their policies and for the eradication of trafficking across the entire globe. It comes from the vision the Lord has placed in her heart.

Vision, as Paul says in Ephesians 3:20, requires imagination. I recently led a prayer meeting with some of our staff, based on Ephesians 1:1–14. We read the passage and reflected on it and then spent some time giving thanks for the good news of Jesus and for the rich inheritance we have as believers. We then prayed for friends or family who aren't yet followers of Jesus, praying that they'd come to know and embrace this good news. We ended by praying for our city, for more and more people to discover how amazing Jesus is. I encouraged everyone to use their imaginations – asking them to picture what it would be like not just for an individual but for a couple, or a whole family, or a number of homes, or even a whole street to start following Jesus. What if this was replicated in a number of streets, or areas of our city? What might this look like, and feel like? It was fascinating hearing the visionary prayers that began to emerge as people began imagining a different future for our city. These kind of prayers are important, helpful and powerful.

When we pray 'big picture' prayers like this, we're actually doing something regal – exercising an authority that in previous generations was reserved for kings, but since the coming of Christ is given to all believers. Kings in the Old Testament were called not to selfishly exercise power, but to use their authority wisely. They were to lead people responsibly. Since Christ, this kingship has passed to all followers of Jesus. We are, as 1 Peter 2:9 says, 'a royal priesthood'. This is not just a nice idea, but a great responsibility that according to Wesley Duewel 'includes our being given a kingly role in our intercession. We become interceding royalty. We, like Jesus, rule and extend Christ's rule by our prevailing intercession . . . He delegates royal authority to us.'[9]

To regularly and effectively pray visionary prayers, you need to sense this royal, God-given responsibility for the matter about which you're praying. You also need to feel compassion for the people and for the circumstances that need changing. I recall once singing a song in church about people returning to the Lord. As I sang the word, I began to pray for our region and for people to turn to the Lord. I was imagining what this looked like, thinking about conversations at meal time, which would start with grace – a prayer of thanks for the food. I was considering people humming songs of praise as they shaved in the morning or did the washing-up. I was imagining the sounds of people in the North turning to the Lord in love, in repentance, in praise. And I found myself weeping, asking the

Lord if I might see more and more of this in my day. God was implanting in my heart something of his heart for the people of my region. This sense of responsibility is common to those who pray visionary prayers – and keep praying them again and again and again.

Some people feel a little uncomfortable praying big visionary prayers. They wonder: is it OK for me to pray like this? Or should this be reserved for very mature or wise Christians? There's nothing in the Bible to suggest that's the case. In fact, when we read the Bible and take note of people who seem to have made a significant impact as they took hold of a God-given vision – like the people of faith listed in Hebrews 11 – we see they were very ordinary people, who prayed bold prayers and took great risks for God. This combination of visionary prayer combined with strategic action is very powerful. But it starts with prayer. That's why Kris Vallotton says: 'Prayer is the catalyst for worldwide transformation. It incites the angels, restrains the darkness, and releases nations into their destiny. It is the key to revival which builds the bridge between what should be and what will be.'[10]

If you've never prayed visionary prayers before and don't know where to start, take some time to consider what you're passionate about. You might like to pray the simple prayer: 'Lord, break my heart for what breaks yours.' It's likely that the Holy Spirit has put inside of you thoughts and dreams of how things could be different, and how his transformative kingdom can impact our world. Start to turn these things into prayer. Perhaps journal about them. It's likely that you'll need to do something in response to your prayers.

So don't be afraid to pray with vision. For yourself. For your family. But even more for your community, city and region. As you read the Bible, use your imagination, and pray with faith for God's future kingdom to be experienced here on earth. We can do this, and must do this, because the human needs are immense and without prayer we won't see the lasting transformation God wants to bring. The Lord is looking for ordinary followers of Jesus who will lift up their voices and begin to cry out to him for change. We can do this because, as Samuel Chadwick said, 'prayer is more important than organisation, more powerful than armies, more influential than wealth, and mightier than all learning'.[11]

> The human needs are immense and without prayer we won't see the lasting transformation God wants to bring.

ACTION: Skim-read this chapter briefly. What's the main thing that stands out for you? What are you going to do about it? Write it down in the space below or in your notebook.

Some people find praying 'big picture' visionary prayers much easier than others. If you find praying like this difficult, acknowledge this, and recognize that you may need to ask the Holy Spirit to stretch your imagination to pray. You may also find that praying creatively helps you. For example, you might find it easier to express your visionary prayers in art rather than word form, maybe drawing or painting the outcome you're longing for the Lord to bring. If that's you, recognize this, and look at your diary to make space in the next few days to give some time creatively to express a visionary prayer for a particular matter that is stirring in your heart.

PRAYER: If you've never prayed visionary prayers before, why not start by praying for a group of Christ-followers? Ask the Holy Spirit to bring to mind who to pray for. It could be your church community. It could be another church known to you. It could be God's wider church family across a whole city, or region, or nation. To help, read Philippians 1:9–11, which is a visionary prayer that Paul prayed for the fledgling church in Philippi. Use his prayer as a means of praying for the group. Pick up phrases from that prayer, and let your prayers develop as you call out to the Lord for these people.

End your prayers by praying for yourself today. Ask the Lord if he wants to give you fresh vision for a particular aspect of your life. Allow your heart to stir and your mind to be stimulated by thoughts and ideas. You might like to write them down in the space below or in your notebook. Then turn them into prayer, asking God to guide you not only in your praying, but also that these things might be turned from vision to action in the coming days and months.

Further Reading:

Mark Batterson, *The Circle Maker* (Grand Rapids, MI: Zondervan, 2012).

$\boxed{\text{W}}$ is for Warfare

When Christ calls us to follow him, we're called into a battle. It's not a battle against people, but against evil forces of darkness that are real and present in the world.

The main way we fight is through prayer. Our prayers are weapons. Weapons for war. That's why **W is for Warfare**.

Many followers of Jesus, especially in the West, know little or nothing of warfare prayers. I still feel like I'm something of a novice at this kind of praying. I realize I have much to learn. But I know that C.S. Lewis was right when he said that 'There is no neutral ground in the universe: every square inch, every split second, is claimed by God and counterclaimed by Satan.'[1] That's why we need to pray warfare prayers.

In one sense, all our prayers are warfare prayers, whether we know it or not. As we pray for God's presence and power and love to be known in the world, in our communities, in our families and in our own lives, so we're praying that the presence of evil and forces of destruction would dissipate and disappear. Samuel Chadwick knew this, saying: 'Satan dreads nothing but prayer. His one concern is to keep the saints from praying. He fears nothing from prayerless studies, prayerless work, prayerless religion. He laughs at our toil, he mocks our wisdom, but he trembles when we pray.'[2] So every prayer is a battle prayer. But there are times when we intentionally pray prayers that

> When Christ calls us to follow him, we're called into a battle.

seek to push back the forces of darkness and see an end to sin and sickness and suffering. That's when we engage in what is sometimes called *spiritual warfare*, and we pray warfare prayers.

In the Bible we've been left a useful model for warfare praying. It's found in Ephesians 6:10–20.

It sets us up for warfare prayers by reminding us in verses 10 to 12 that there is an enemy – sometimes called 'the devil' or Satan[3] – who has 'schemes' to frustrate God's people and his kingdom plans. Our 'struggle' is with him, not human beings, and 'against the rulers, against the authorities, against the powers of this dark world and against the spiritual forces of evil in the heavenly realms'. This description of some of the forces of darkness tells us that there's a battle going on in the spirit realm. Who we are, how we live and the way we pray affect this battle. God wants us to be strong and to stand in this battle, whereas the enemy wants us to fall.

> There's a battle going on in the spirit realm. Who we are, how we live and the way we pray affect this battle.

The way to stand firm is to make sure we're clothed in Christ, wearing his armour. Various pieces of armour are mentioned in Ephesians 6:13–17 that we're given when we start following Jesus, but we mustn't forget there's a daily need to put on God's armour. Every day we need to be clothed with Christ so we can pray and live for him. Most of the armour listed is defensive: like 'the breastplate of righteousness' guarding our heart and 'the helmet of salvation' defending our minds. Two main weapons of attack are mentioned. One is 'the sword of the Spirit, which is the word of God'. As we declare the truth of God's word in speech and particularly in action, so the kingdom of God is advanced. The other is prayer. Prayer is what we're supposed to do once we're armour-ready, which is why, having listed the various pieces of armour and the sword, Ephesians 6:18–20 says:

> And pray in the Spirit on all occasions with all kinds of prayer and requests. With this in mind, be alert and always keep on praying for all the Lord's people. Pray also for me . . . that I will fearlessly make known the mystery of the gospel, for which I am an ambassador . . .

Here we're given some specific guidance on warfare praying that we'd do well to heed.

First, we're to pray *guided by the Holy Spirit*. 'Pray in the Spirit' is the phrase used. Some say this means praying in tongues. Praying in tongues is one of the main ways we 'pray in the Spirit' (see **T is for Tongues**), but the phrase means more than that because we're told to 'pray in the Spirit . . . with *all kinds* of prayers and requests' (emphasis mine). That means any kind of prayer that is Spirit-inspired. So tongues would be one important means of praying 'in the Spirit' but, depending on the situation, it could include intercession (see **I is for Intercession**), or prophetic declaration (see **P is for Prophetic**), or perhaps corporate confession (see **C is for Confession**) and more. The Spirit will guide us and show us how to pray, if we ask him. So ask.

Second, we're to pray *relentless prayers* (see **R is for Relentless**). We're to keep going and persevere. That's why we're told 'always keep on praying'. Warfare prayer is not normally done in two minutes. It requires tenacity and hard work. When we're tempted to give up, we need to press on and press in. We'll need to encourage each other in this, looking out for the ones who are floundering, and hold them up. It's all part of being God's army, praying warfare prayers.

Third, we're to pray *for those working on the front line.* In Ephesians 6:20 they're called Christ's 'ambassadors'. This includes evangelists – which is why Paul says 'Pray . . . for me' but it includes others too, who are representing and re-presenting Christ to those around them. Such people are especially vulnerable to attacks of the enemy and need our prayers.

When I think of a follower of Jesus who prays warfare prayers, I think of Jonathan Oloyede. Jonathan is an inspired and committed man of prayer, has played a huge role in the recent Global Day of Prayer and is now convenor of the National Day of Prayer and Worship. Jonathan has spoken at The Belfrey and I've heard him pray, and I know him to be a man who cries out to God and seeks to push back the kingdom of darkness through his warfare prayers.

Some people, when they pray warfare prayers, speak to the devil and forces of darkness and rebuke them. There is a place for this. Jesus did this sometimes when confronting evil and the demonic, especially when praying for individuals. However, the main way the Bible encourages us to pray warfare prayers is to pray to God, and ask him to move in power.[4] This is how the first disciples prayed in Acts 4 when their gospel message was opposed.[5] As we pray to him and praise him, so he sends his angelic forces to fight against the enemy.

Daniel the prophet is a Bible character who discovered that God loves to send angels in response to warfare prayers. Daniel 9 records his great prayer where he says to God: 'Lord, listen! Lord, forgive! Lord, hear and act! For your sake . . . do not delay . . .'[6] In the next chapter he's given a vision and in the context of fasting, he then encounters a man who is possibly

Christ but more likely a mighty angel of God. This man then speaks to him about his prayers, telling him that as soon as he prayed, his prayers were heard and responded to, but there was a delay because of a demonic battle that took place in the spiritual realm for twenty-one days. This tells us not only why the answer to our prayers might sometimes be delayed, but also that God hears our prayers straight away and that they have the capacity to summon angelic hosts.

Praising, as well as praying, can also cause angelic beings to gather. We see this in some of the wars recorded in the Old Testament. These wars were physical battles against human enemies. Since Christ and his victory over sin and death at the cross, we're no longer called to wage war like that.[7] As we've seen, our warfare is now through prayer and loving action. But there's still much to learn from these Old Testament battles about spiritual warfare, and one thing we discover is that the singers and worship leaders often went out at the front of the army.[8] Praise prepared the ground for warfare. It's the same as we engage in spiritual warfare today: our praise of God opens the way for effective and decisive warfare prayer.

God wants to train us for warfare prayer. King David, who was a warrior king, knew this. In Psalm 144 he prays: 'Praise be to the LORD my Rock, who trains my hand for war . . .'[9] As we apply this to spiritual warfare, it's a reminder that such training may well be demanding and take time. We need to learn from seasoned prayer warriors what it is to pray, fast and see God's kingdom advance here on earth, using the weapons of faithful prayer coupled with humble living[10] and loving those who are against us.[11]

All this warfare praying also needs to be worked out in our everyday lives. There are lots of ways to do this, as we seek to be people who not only 'pray in the Spirit' but also 'walk in the Spirit'.[12] The artist Charity Bowman Webb puts it like this: 'If you have ever walked through an armoury of the Spirit, the weapons may have surprised you. Among the classic swords and shields did anyone happen to see a song, a paint brush or a dancers shoe, a skillful spreadsheet, an architect's plan or a business strategy?'[13]

Warfare prayer, combined with practical action is the strategy of transformation.

ACTION: Did you realize that your prayers can help and influence the spiritual battle taking place in the heavenly realm? What does this make you think about your prayers?

Read the story of Daniel's encounter with the angel in Daniel 10:7–19. What do you make of this? Write down your reflections in the space below or in your notebook.

PRAYER: Thank God that as a follower of Christ, you're given armour to wear. Go through each item of the armour in Ephesians 6:10–17 and, in prayer, put them on, recognizing that you're clothed for battle.

Now ask the Lord to bring to mind a situation that feels like a battle. Begin to talk to God in prayer about it. Ask the Holy Spirit to guide you so you can pray 'in the Spirit' for this. Allow your prayers to rise up and ask the Lord to come and fight against the enemy, bringing his transformative kingdom of power and love.

End by thanking God that Christ won the greatest victory of all on the cross, and that there will be a day when there will be no more fighting – physically or spiritually. Pray for that day to come soon.

Further Reading:

R. Arthur Mathews, *Born for Battle* (Sevenoaks: OMF, 2011). Kindle edition.

.

$\boxed{\text{X}}$ is for eXamen

Living a prayerful life, as we've seen, means practising the presence of God all the time. As we do this, we will also find that we want to have focused times to pray, like first thing in the morning. As well as this, many Christ-followers have also found that it's good to take some time at the end of the day to pray, before we sleep. There are lots of ways we can do this, one of which is to use a form of prayer known as the *Examen*. That's why **X is for eXamen**.

The Examen is a technique of prayerful reflection on the events of the day. The aim is to recognize God's presence and discern his direction in our lives. The Examen is an ancient practice in the church that can help us see God's hand at work in every aspect of our lives. Pioneered by Ignatius of Loyola[1] who founded the Jesuit movement, this model of prayer has been especially used by Roman Catholic Christians, but is increasingly used by other traditions in God's church too.[2]

The word *examen* has its origins in Latin and means 'examination'. It's not the kind of examination you do at school, which is a test. It's an examination – a careful looking at – the day that has passed.[3]

My friend Mark Miller, who's a gifted church leader in Stockton-on-Tees, uses the Examen at the end of most days. He's told me how it helps him not only grow in his relationship with Christ, but also become much more self-aware, recognizing his strengths and weaknesses, and his need for the abiding, transforming presence of Christ.

Here's a simple five-step version of the Examen[4] that is easy to use and based on five Rs.

1. *Recognize God's presence.*

Look back on the events of the day in the company of the Holy Spirit. The day may seem confusing to you – a blur, a jumble, a muddle. Ask God to shine the light of his presence, bringing clarity and understanding.

2. *Revere God, with much gratitude.*

Worship God for who he is, and for his caring presence through the day. Gratitude (see **G is for Gratitude**) is the foundation of our relationship with God. Consider your day in the presence of God and note its joys and delights. Focus on the day's gifts. Look at the work you did, the people you interacted with. What did you receive from these people? What did you give them? Pay attention to small things – the food you ate, the sights you saw, and other seemingly small pleasures, and be thankful.

3. *Review the day, noting your emotions.*

One of Ignatius's great insights was that we detect the presence of the Spirit of God in the movements of our emotions. Walk through the day in detail and reflect on the feelings you experienced. Boredom? Elation? Resentment? Compassion? Anger? Confidence? What is God saying through these feelings? Take note of anything you regret. But look deeply for other implications. Does a feeling of frustration perhaps mean that God wants you to consider a new direction in some area of your work? Are you concerned about a friend? Perhaps you should reach out to them in some way.

4. *Repent of sin and pray from it.*

Ask the Holy Spirit to direct you to something during the day that God thinks is particularly important, especially anywhere you fell short, or something that needs putting right. Take note of one sin or fault. It may be linked to a feeling or a significant encounter with another person. You may be guided to something that seems rather insignificant, but allow your mind to focus on it. Pray about it. Make sure you say sorry to God for wrong thoughts, words or actions. Allow the prayers to arise spontaneously from your heart – so that out of confession you pray prayers of supplication (for yourself) and intercession (for others).

5. **Respond** *by choosing to do something now, and by preparing well for tomorrow.*

Resolve to act rightly in the day ahead. Chose one thing, even if it's very small, that you'll do differently tomorrow. Consider what's coming up. Are you doubtful? Cheerful? Apprehensive? Full of delighted anticipation? Allow these feelings to turn into prayer. Seek God's guidance. Ask him for help and understanding. Pray for hope. End by praying *The Lord's Prayer*.

King Solomon was someone we read of in the Bible who practised this kind of prayerful self-reflection. He sought to do so in the presence of God, encouraging his people by saying:

> Guard your heart, for everything you do flows from it.
> Keep your mouth free of perversity;
> keep corrupt talk from your lips.
> Let your eyes look straight ahead,
> fix your gaze directly before you.
> Give careful thought to the paths for your feet
> and be steadfast in your ways.[5]

He continued to do this, even later in life as he struggled with the consequences of some of his poor decision-making, saying:

'Do not be quick with your mouth, do not be hasty in your heart to utter anything before God. God is in heaven and you are on earth, so let your words be few.'[6]

While it's good not to rush this kind of reflective praying, it doesn't have to take long. As we regularly look back through the day and learn to see God's hand at work, so this kind of prayer can become a normal and helpful end to our day. It's good for us and, like all praying, brings pleasure to God. King David describes our praying – especially in the evening – as like a sweet-smelling aroma of incense rising to God, which he loves to receive.[7] It also sets us up well for sleep and settles us so that the Lord can continue to be at work within us as we sleep (see **N is for Night**).

> King David describes our praying – especially in the evening – as like a sweet-smelling aroma of incense rising to God, which he loves to receive.

There may be times when we use the Examen and recognize strong emotions that have stirred up in us during the day. This might be sadness or anger or frustration, or happiness or elation or wonder. At the very least it's good to recognize these emotions and entrust them to the Lord. Sometimes we might need to take longer to reflect on them and to hear how God is speaking to us through them. If we come to the end of the day feeling negative and pessimistic it can also be helpful to look back and notice the goodness of God that might have been eclipsed in some of the day's more trying circumstances. To reflect and pray in this way involves using the imagination, and talking with Jesus as a friend and being honest about what has happened (see **H is for Honesty**). Those who use the Examen, or some kind of similar way of praying at the end of the day, say that God often highlights seemingly insignificant moments and uses them to help give direction to their lives.

Eugene Peterson was a prayerful pastor who understood the benefit of all kinds of prayer, including this kind of reflective end-of-the-day prayer. He discovered over many years of praying, that: 'Prayer enlarges our imagination and makes us grateful, joyful participants in what has been and is yet to come.'[8] So make sure that you start – and end – the day, with prayer.

ACTION: Do you pray before you sleep? If so, what kind of prayers do you pray? Have you found this beneficial?

What stands out for you in this chapter? Is the Examen something you've used? Is there an aspect of it that you'd like to try? Commit to praying the Examen tonight, if you can.

PRAYER: It's now the end of the day. Use the five-step model set out in this chapter:
1) Recognize God's presence.
2) Revere God, with much gratitude.
3) Review the day, noting your emotions.
4) Repent of sin and pray from it.
5) Respond by choosing to do something now, and by preparing well for tomorrow.

End by asking the Lord to continue to be at work in you as you sleep and close by praying *The Lord's Prayer*.

Further Reading:

Jim Manney, *A Simple, Life-Changing Prayer: Discovering the Power of St Ignatius Loyola's Examen* (Chicago, IL: Loyola Press, 2011).

$\boxed{\text{Y}}$ is for Yearning

There are times when followers of Jesus sense a strong need to spend time in God's presence, seeking the Lord and calling out to him for someone or something. We might even find it hard to articulate exactly what this is or how it feels; we just know we need to pray. Some saints of old have called this 'travailing in prayer' whilst others have described it as having 'a burden to pray'. This need to cry out to God is like a weight we're carrying, which is usually lifted after a time of significant prayer. Sometimes this need to pray feels like it's coming from somewhere deep within. It creates a stirring and a hunger to pray. The soul yearns to converse with God. That's why **Y is for Yearning**.

Richard Dearden, who heads up Prophetic Ministry at The Belfrey knows about this kind of prayer. He prays daily about all sorts of things, but there are times and seasons when a particular prayer need grips him, or he feels the Holy Spirit asking him simply to seek the Lord more intentionally and passionately. He might not even understand why, but he knows he needs to pray. He just yearns to pray and that desire is only satisfied by giving time to pray.

It's likely that this is what the apostle Paul was referring to when he said that 'the Spirit helps us in our weakness. We do not know what we ought to pray for, but the Spirit himself intercedes for us through wordless groans' or, as The Passion Translation puts it, 'with emotional sighs too deep for words'.[1]

These groans can sometimes be strong, sometimes feeling not unlike the labour pains of a pregnant woman. It's fascinating that some of the female intercessors during the Hebridean awakening in Scotland in the 1950s described sensations in prayer when God's Spirit would come upon them and they would feel struggle and pain. They knew their prayers were helping new souls become birthed into God's kingdom.[2]

Many of the biblical prophets knew about this kind of yearning prayer, with their prophetic revelation sometimes emerging out of such prayer times. Isaiah the prophet says in prayer to God: '. . . we wait for you; your name and renown are the desire of our hearts. My soul yearns for you in the night; in the morning my spirit longs for you.'[3] He knows he needs to pursue God and spend time waiting in his presence, seeking him in prayer. King David writes something similar in Psalm 63:

> You, God are my God,
> earnestly I seek you:
> I thirst for you,
> my whole being longs for you,
> in a dry and weary land
> where there is no water.[4]

This kind of seeking after God is sometimes described as 'waiting' for him. This is not a passive waiting, like waiting for a bus to come. No, it's a very active waiting, much like a night-time sentry – a 'watchman'[5] – who if they're doing their job properly won't be sitting around aimlessly but will be alert and active in making sure all is safe and well. In fact, the waiting is part of the prayer. It's all part of seeking the Lord with passion and vigour. People who yearn for God in prayer and seek him in this way are sometimes waiting for guidance and prophetic direction. Sometimes they're waiting for an answer. Sometimes they're waiting for peace. Sometimes they're crying out to God in intercession for a situation that they feel they can't stop praying about (see **R is for Relentless**) until the burden lifts.

Those who aren't used to this kind of prayer might ask what this feels like, or how you know when the burden lifts. It's hard to be precise, as this kind of yearning prayer can take various forms. Like all prayer, it's all about relationship. People pray like this because the Spirit of Jesus stirs their heart. As we develop and grow in our relationship with God, some will sense the need to pray yearning prayers fairly regularly, whilst for others it may be just occasionally.

Sometimes this kind of prayer can be felt by one but shared and practised by many – for example, by a church or Christian community. When my Grandpa Luther was studying at Cliff College in the 1920s, all the students were woken up one night and asked to gather. The principal, Samuel Chadwick told them that one of the students had been taken very ill and he felt a yearning for the whole college to pray. So he asked everyone in the college to go back to their rooms and kneel down and pray. He told them they should not get off their knees until they had a clear sense from the Lord that their prayers for healing had been answered. This they all did. Next morning at breakfast Chadwick announced to the college that the student was well, and together they thanked the Lord for answering their prayers.

All this means that prayer meetings – especially if they contain people burdened with yearning prayers – might not always be the gentle, quiet occasions that some expect! It may be very appropriate for prayer gatherings to include people who pray with passion and intensity, who cry (literally)[6] for situations as the compassion of God takes hold of them. Some might feel the need to stand, or pace around, or lie down on the floor, or kneel, or lift their hands. Others might want to be creative and paint their prayerful groanings, expressing them in art, or sculpture, or music, or dance. I have been in prayer meetings where someone starts to pray yearning prayers, and as a result others in the room – and sometimes the whole room – seem to capture something of the groaning of the first person. The yearning becomes corporate as the Spirit of God takes hold of a group of people, burdening them to cry out in intercession for something that is on the heart of God.

The Holy Spirit can place all kinds of prayer burdens on our hearts. Given that God longs for all people to come to know Jesus Christ,[7] it's not surprising that sometimes the yearning is for people to start following Jesus. John Welch was a minister of Anwoth in Scotland in the late sixteenth century and would often get up in the middle of the night, groaning in prayer for the conversion of people in his community. He would wrap himself in a blanket to stay warm and then intercede for the men and women of his parish. When his wife would beg him to go back to sleep, he would say, 'I have the souls of three thousand to answer for and I know not how it is with many of them.'[8]

This sounds similar to the prayer yearning of Isaiah 26:9 which, as we've seen, sometimes comes not just in the day but also at night (see **N is for Night**). This happens to me occasionally. I awaken with a sense of needing to pray about something or someone. The urge to pray is so strong I usually find I can't go back to sleep until I've prayed. At times that might be just for a few minutes, but sometimes much longer.

I was praying with a woman at the end of a service recently at The Belfrey, and as we prayed I sensed the Lord calling her to a deeper level of intercession. I spoke this over her, and as I did so I said that I expected the Lord would start waking her up in the night with a strong urge to pray about things, and that she shouldn't be surprised by this. At the end of the prayer time, I was encouraged by her telling me that just the previous night she'd awoken three times with a deep desire to pray for various matters and that it would only recede when she'd devoted a good time to pray.

To yearn in prayer is a humble but beautiful activity of God's people. It's sharing his concern for someone or something. It often involves our emotions – perhaps feeling God's love, but maybe sensing his pain. To share in the work of God through prayer in this way is an honour and privilege.

To yearn in prayer is a humble but beautiful activity of God's people. It's sharing his concern for someone or something.

ACTION: Is yearning prayer something you've ever experienced? Write about it in the space below or in your notebook. If you're new to this, do you know anyone else who sometimes prays this way? Again, write your reflections below.

Is there anything particular you need to do, in response to reading this chapter? If so, write it down (below or in your notebook) to remind you.

PRAYER: Welcome the presence of God. After spending some time in devotion, thank him that he uses ordinary people, like you, to change the world through prayer and action. Now invite him to take you deeper into prayer. You might like to ask him to use you in yearning prayer in the coming days and months, urging you to pray for things that are particularly important to him. It's possible that he might respond immediately to that prayer, and you're stirred to pray yearning prayers right now! However, it may be that such groaning begins to grow in the days ahead, especially as you come face to face with people or situations that need transformation, and the Spirit of God places a burden of prayer upon you. Be open. Be ready. And thank the Lord for the gift of prayer.

Further Reading:

Wesley L. Duewel, *Mighty Prevailing Prayer* (Grand Rapids, MI: Zondervan, 1990).

$\boxed{Z}$ is for Zero

This A–Z is all about prayer. It's about building strong foundations for daily conversations with God. We've seen that there are lots of ways to pray, and that there are multiple benefits of praying. But what happens if we don't pray? What about the prayerless life? What happens when there is zero prayer? That's why **Z is for Zero**.

Prayer should be at the heart of the relationship that a Christ-follower has with God. Prayer is what we do. That means that it should become part and parcel of the life of a Christ-follower and normative at Christian gatherings. We pray, acknowledging the Lord and welcoming his presence. As is sometimes said, he's the unseen but welcome guest.

> Prayer should be at the heart of the relationship that a Christ-follower has with God. Prayer is what we do.

I remember when I was training to be a church leader in Oxford, I did a monthly placement in what seemed to me to be a very quiet and sleepy village in the quiet Cotswolds countryside. The church leader was soon to retire and seemed rather slow and unproductive. In my youthful enthusiasm I wasn't sure if there was much I could learn from this leader and his dozy parish. Fairly early on in my time there, when we were eating together one lunchtime, the phone rang and he took the call. He listened and ended by saying, 'OK, we will pray.' I expected he would add the situation to his prayer list, or perhaps we'd pray about it after lunch. But to my surprise he told me to stop eating, and he then explained the prayer need and said we would pray there and then. I was taken aback, especially as the hot lunch was rather tasty and might well go cold if the prayer went on too long! This didn't seem to bother him at all. Instead, he launched into prayer, calling out to the Lord for the person in question, and then encouraging me to do the same. I soon discovered that behind this elderly gentleman was a lifetime of rich prayer. It was the most normal and natural thing for him to do. I was humbled, realizing I had much to learn.

Since then I've sought to do what the Bible says in Colossians 4:2, which is to 'Devote yourselves to prayer'. I know I still have much to work on, but that is my desire and my intent, because I know that prayer is key to discipleship. I know that prayer strengthens me. It's cheesy but true that 'seven days without prayer makes one weak'! I also know that prayer works. I know that prayer changes things. Basically, I know I need to pray.

There's a close link between prayer and presence. We pray because God is here and present. And yet when we pray, God still comes. As I say in *A–Z of Discipleship,* 'The Holy Spirit loves to be invited, which is why one of the most ancient prayers of the church is "Come, Holy Spirit." To invoke and welcome the Spirit doesn't mean that he was not present before. It simply means that we are asking him to come in greater measure, manifesting his presence to a greater degree.'[1] That means that when we don't pray, God is not absent.[2] He's still here – just a prayer away. And he's wanting to get our attention, and hoping to be called upon.

Surveys show that most people pray. Whether they live in the East or West, whether they're rich or poor, young or old, most people pray. They may not be followers of Jesus. They may be uncertain of what they believe. They may not be sure if there's even a God at all. But they pray. At least a bit. Perhaps they ask for help when there's a crisis. Maybe they find themselves giving thanks when something has gone well. This shouldn't surprise us, because human beings are made for relationship with God, so when we pray we're actually doing what we were created for.

There are a few people who don't pray at all. They've never prayed, or they did once and didn't see the benefit so they've stopped. Their life is now prayerless. Of course God still loves those who have zero prayer in their lives. He's not given up on them and still desires relationship with them. But such a prayerless life closes a door to God and creates a barrier. The Bible describes a number of results of this.

One is that the God who is present feels distant. Prayerlessness, according to Wesley Duewel, 'robs you of the awareness of the smile on His face, of the blessedness of listening to His voice. It robs you of the touch of his hand upon you and of much of His guidance. It robs you of his power.'[3] This sense of God being far away was the experience of the first humans when they chose to disobey God and stopped talking to him.[4] Prayerlessness is normally a sign of a failing, dying or nonexistent relationship with God.[5]

Another result is that the personal benefits that come to us when we pray are no longer received. The prayerless person will lack many things that God longs to give, simply because they don't pray. As James says: 'You do not have because you do not ask God.'[6] For example, the person who stops praying does not enjoy God's forgiveness. God speaks about this to the prayerless people of Israel through the prophet Isaiah in chapter 43, describing how he longs for them to know their sins are for-given, but this is not their experience because 'You have not called on me'.[7]

A further result of prayerlessness is a greater openness to temptation. Temptation comes to all people. It's not a sin to be tempted, it's how we respond to it that matters. It's good to avoid temptation if possible,[8] and best only to enter into it in the power of the Spirit, as Jesus did.[9] But when we stop praying, we're much more prone to temptation. Jesus says just this, telling his disciples: 'Watch and pray so that you will not fall into temptation.'[10] We face many battles unnecessarily brought on by prayerlessness.

A life of zero prayer soon leads to a life without God. Ac-cording to Duewel, people who don't pray 'are rarely used by God. Prayerlessness means unavailability to God.'[11] No longer is the Lord referenced and the Bible no longer provides a moral compass. People then end up doing 'as they [see] fit'[12] which often results in selfishness and ethical decline. The prophet Zephaniah sees this happening to the people in his day, saying of Jerusalem that 'She obeys no one, she accepts no correction. She does not trust in the LORD, she does not draw near to her God'[13] which then results in poor decision-making, bad leader-ship, and unjust behaviour that 'knows no shame'.[14]

Individuals and communities that live this way are, in the end, heading for a fall. When we ignore God and remove our-selves from him, then our destiny is destruction. The story of the Bible describes this time and time again, with Jesus saying: 'If you do not remain in me, you are like a branch that is thrown away and withers; such branches are picked up, thrown into the fire and burned.'[15] This is not God's desire and it's why he sent Jesus, not only to bring forgiveness for the consequences of go-ing our own way, but also to empower us to live differently and live life well, in a prayerful relationship with God. That's why it's good to pray, and to encourage others to do the same.

When people who aren't yet followers of Jesus talk to me about faith and church, I often ask them about prayer and I encourage them to pray. That's because I know that when people start praying, things start to change. Even the most tentative prayer can begin to nudge open a door in our hearts, releasing the Spirit of God to work. That's why when I visit a home, I will pray. When I visit someone in hospital, I will pray. When I talk with someone on the street and they share a need or something they're thankful for, I will pray. When I'm prompted by the Spirit, I will pray. I'm learning that nothing of lasting significance happens without prayer.

> Even the most tentative prayer can begin to nudge open a door in our hearts, releasing the Spirit of God to work.

Many followers of Jesus in the West have still to grasp this. They might pray a bit, perhaps because they feel they should. But what is needed is something more. Something deeper. A proper conversation with God. The believers in Laodicea in the book of Revelation were rather like this, which is why the risen Christ said to them, 'Here I am! I stand at the door and knock',[16] inviting them into a closer relationship of prayer with them. But many don't respond to this call to become people of prayer. This, says Samuel Chadwick is 'because of its cost. The cost is not so much in the sweat of agonising supplication, as in the daily fidelity to the life of prayer. It is the acid test of devotion. Nothing in the life of faith is so difficult to maintain.'[17] That's why we need to be honest about our struggles in prayer (see **H is for Honesty**), and also encourage each other to pray, especially in the hard times.

Sometimes followers of Jesus go through a tough patch. Circumstances might be difficult (see **S is for Sad**). Prayers might not seem to be answered (see **U is for Unanswered**). God might feel distant. When that's happened to me there are three things that I don't feel like doing. I don't feel like reading the Bible. I don't feel like I want to spend time in worship with other believers. And I don't feel like praying. What I've discovered, though, is that those are the three things that it would be best for me to do, because they're the things that will help me the most!

When we feel distant from God like this, the Lord is kind and compassionate. There is no shame in struggling with prayer. It happens to us all. In fact, as Jim Cymbala says, 'God is attracted to weakness. He can't resist those who humbly and honestly admit how desperately they need him.'[18] So what's needed when we've stopped praying is for us to restart. This might begin with a friend praying for us and with us. It might start with just speaking out a sentence of prayer. Or maybe finding some paper and drawing your prayer. Or writing it down. The most important thing is to pray.

God longs for us to know him. So he calls us to pray. And he wants to transform the world through our prayers, which is why he says:

> If my people, who are called by my name, will humble themselves and pray and seek my face and turn from their wicked ways, then I will hear from heaven, and I will forgive their sin and will heal their land.[19]

If we want to see individuals, families, cities, regions and nations transformed, we must pray. What's wonderful is that the

Spirit of Jesus is inviting us to pray. The question is whether we will respond to the call.

'It would seem', wrote my grandfather's mentor,[20] Samuel Chadwick, that 'the biggest thing in God's universe is a man who prays. There is only one thing more amazing, and that is, that man, knowing this, should not pray . . . In the estimate of God, prayer is more wonderful than all the wonders of the heavens, more glorious than all the mysteries of the earth, more mighty than all the forces of creation.'[21]

So let us pray.

ACTION: Was there a time in your life when you didn't pray? If so, what was it like? Did, as this chapter suggests, God feel distant? Write about it in the space below or in your notebook.

What about now? Hopefully, helped by this *A–Z of Prayer*, you're praying and discovering some of the benefits of prayer. Is that right? What has stood out for you on this journey you've been on as you've read this short book on prayer? Again, write down some of your reflections.

PRAYER: Spend some time thanking God for all you've been discovering about prayer.

Now ask him to take you further and deeper. Pray that you would know him more, as you pray. Ask that you might see more answers to your prayers and be able to share them with others.

Close by asking the Lord to help you encourage someone else to pray, especially someone who's not yet a follower of Jesus. You might want to give them a copy of this *A–Z of Prayer*, or perhaps *A–Z of Discipleship* to start them off. Pray for the guidance of God's Spirit in this, and then be obedient to what he's asking of you.

Further Reading:

Jim Cymbala, *Fresh Wind, Fresh Fire* (Grand Rapids, MI: Zondervan, 1997, 2003).

Afterword

It may be you've read, or skim-read this book on prayer and feel overwhelmed. Maybe you've seen that there's more to prayer than you thought, and rather than exciting you to dive deep into the depths of prayer, instead you feel unsure even about dipping your toe in the shallow end!

If that's you, just start. Start somewhere. And start simple. Just start talking to God. Why not begin with an aspect of prayer that interests you, and go from there? If you need a model to help you, start with *The Lord's Prayer,* with the structure explained in **E is for Extemporary**, or use the *thank you, sorry, please* tool also mentioned in that chapter.

> Start somewhere. And start simple. Just start talking to God.

Also, in your early days of praying, close your eyes and speak your prayers out loud. If you've never done either of those things they'll probably feel strange at first, but you'll soon get over them, and in a world of many distractions, they'll help you stay focused.

Many followers of Jesus find it really helpful to pray with others. So do consider joining with two or three friends to pray together regularly, perhaps every two weeks. As well as praying for all sorts of things together, you'll find that through praying with others you'll learn much and grow significantly as a person of prayer.

Crucially, make sure you're part of a local church family, and prioritize attending the church prayer meeting. You'll begin to see over time that prayer really does change things.

Also, be aware that you don't have to practise all the kinds of prayer described in this book all at once! Some are basic (like adoration, confession, gratitude and intercession) to the prayer life of all disciples, whereas you might practise others at particular times and seasons in your life. This is fine and normal. As we grow in our relationship with God, certain practices become more helpful for a while, and there's always more to discover. It's rather like we add to the armoury of prayer, becoming better equipped by the Spirit of Jesus for work and prayer in God's kingdom.

So pray. And keep praying. Be someone building strong foundations for daily conversations with God.

If you have found this book
helpful, you may wish to read:

A-Z of Discipleship

*Building strong foundations for
a life of following Jesus*

Matthew Porter

978-1-78078-456-4

Notes

Preface

[1] 'A kingdom-of-heaven life consists of things to do and things to think, but if there is no prayer at the center nothing lives. Prayer is the heart that pumps blood into all the words and acts. Prayer is not just one more thing in an inventory of elements that make up a following-Jesus, kingdom-of-heaven life. Prayer is the heart. If there is no heart doing its work from the center, no matter how precise the words, no matter how perfectly formed the actions, there is only a corpse.' Eugene H. Peterson, *The Word Made Flesh* (London: Hodder & Stoughton, 2008), p. 167.

[2] If we are to see lives changed in our day, then: 'We must learn to pray, and we must pray to learn to pray.' Leonard Ravenhill, *Why Revival Tarries* (Bloomington, MN: Bethany House, 1959, 1987), p. 150.

[3] 'I am convinced that the return to prayer, the rediscovery of prayer, is the most urgent and important concern in our twenty-first century world.' Johannes Hartl, *Heart Fire* (Edinburgh: Muddy Pearl, 2018), p. 4.

Introduction

1 Clement of Alexandria (c.150–215AD) – cited in https://www
   .osv.com/OSVNewsweekly/Story/TabId/2672/ArtMID/13567/
   ArticleID/9025/Start-conversing-with-Jesus.aspx (accessed 9.11.18).
2 Jesus told a helpful story about prayer that's recorded in Luke 18.
   The writer of Luke tells us (in v. 1) why he did this: 'Jesus told
   his disciples a parable to show them that they should always pray
   and not give up.'
3 Romans 8:34.
4 Romans 8:26–27.

A is for Adoration

1 See Matthew 6:9.
2 Samuel Chadwick, writing in the 1930s, agrees saying: 'Let the
   first act be to affirm the fact of the Holy Presence . . . I think in
   adoring love and wonder of His Character and Attributes, of His
   Majesty and Might, of His Grace and Glory . . . I never take any
   book but the Bible into the secret place. It is my Prayer-Book.'
   Samuel Chadwick, *The Path of Prayer* (London: Hodder &
   Stoughton, 1931), p. 33.
3 As Sir Henry Lunn says: 'our instinct tells us that we must begin our prayer with Adoration. As we realise into Whose presence
   we have come, Adoration becomes inevitable'. See Lunn's classic
   book on prayer *The Secret of the Saints* (Cambridge: W. Heffer &
   Sons Ltd., 1933), p. 76.
4 See 1 John 4:19.
5 Cited in ed. Rodney Wallace Kennedy and Derek C. Hatch, *Gathering Together: Baptists at Work in Worship* (Eugene, OR: Pickwick
   Publications, 2013), p. 153.
6 Cited in Archbishop Doye T. Agama, *An Apostolic Handbook Vol-
   ume Three: Ancient Prayers of the First Apostles and the Early Church*
   (Peterborough: Upfront Publishing, 2015), p. 75.

[7] See e.g. Psalm 136.

[8] See Exodus 20:1–4.

[9] Mark 12:30.

[10] Beni Johnson, *The Happy Intercessor* (Shippensburg, PA: Destiny Image, 2009), p. 120.

[11] See James 4:8: 'Draw near to God, and he will draw near to you', ESV.

[12] 1 Kings 8:23.

[13] See Revelation 4:10–11.

[14] See Psalm 63:4.

[15] See Psalm 95:6.

[16] This is sometimes called *prostration* or *lying prostrate*. See e.g. Nehemiah 8:6.

[17] See Psalm 47:1.

[18] See Psalm 149:3.

B is for Belief

[1] See Luke 11:1.

[2] See Matthew 6:5.

[3] See Hebrews 11:6.

[4] Like many churches, The Belfrey offers 'prayer ministry' at our services. Prayer Ministry is praying with someone for the Holy Spirit to come. When someone requests such prayer it usually involves laying on hands and often there are two (or occasionally more) people praying.

[5] See e.g. Matthew 9:22.

[6] See e.g. Mark 9:16ff and Matthew 13:58.

[7] See Hebrew 11:1.

[8] Jesus said that one of the characteristics God is looking for in his people is 'faith' – see Luke 18:8.

[9] See Luke 8:43–48.

[10] See Luke 5:17–20.

[11] See Matthew 17:20.

[12] Matthew Porter, *A–Z of Discipleship* (Milton Keynes: Authentic, 2017), p. 36.

[13] See John 4:39–42.

[14] See e.g. Psalm 126:5–6, which in *The Message* begins with: 'And now, GOD, do it again – bring rains to our drought-stricken lives . . .'

[15] See e.g.: https://www.futurity.org/brains-speech-writing-communication-919852/ (accessed 9.11.18).

[16] As the first disciples did – see Luke 17:5.

C is for Confession

[1] See e.g. Isaiah 43:25.

[2] This is explained in some detail in Hebrews chapters 4 to 10.

[3] For many it is a liberating experience, often initially involving tears of confession. For some it is an uncomfortable experience, as they come face to face with their own sinfulness. This was true of Simon (in Luke 5:1–11) when he felt unworthy in the presence of Jesus and said, 'Go away from me, Lord; I am a sinful man!'

[4] Jesus tells a simple and helpful story about this in Luke 18:10–13, describing two people praying. The one who receives forgiveness is the humble one who in this story is the disliked tax collector, who prays: 'God, have mercy on me, a sinner.'

[5] Luke 11:4. See Matthew 6:10–12, which includes the words 'Give us today our daily bread', implying that the prayer should be prayed every day.

[6] 1 John 1:9; 2:1–2.

[7] See e.g. Matthew 6:9–13.

[8] See John 16:8.

[9] See Romans 8:31.

[10] See Romans 8:1.

[11] See James 5:16.

[12] When someone confesses sin to us, it's crucial that confidence is kept. However, some criminal matters need to be disclosed to

the police or other appropriate bodies, so if asked, 'Can I share something in total confidence?' it's important to answer something like, 'Of course, although you need to know that I have a duty to disclose some matters of a criminal nature.'

[13] Psalm 51:7–12.

D is for Devotion

[1] See Luke 10:38–42.
[2] Oswald Chambers, *My Utmost For His Highest* (New York: Dodd, Mead & Co, 1963), p. 219.
[3] Psalm 27:4,8.
[4] Pete Greig, *Dirty Glory* (Carol Stream, IL: NavPress 2016; London: Hodder & Stoughton, 2018), p. 54.
[5] Johannes Hartl, op. cit., p. 189.

E is for Extemporary

[1] Bible translators today believe passionately that all peoples should be able to read the Bible in their 'heart-language', that is, using their everyday conversational means of speech. Many people speak or read more than one language and so can still read it even if there is no Bible in their mother tongue. However, it normally does not have the same impact as reading it in their heart-language. It is the same in prayer. It's best to pray from the heart, using our heart-language.
[2] https://www.churchofengland.org/our-faith/going-church-and-praying/lords-prayer (accessed 22.11.18). Based on Matthew 6:9–13.
[3] Ed. William Porter, *For Noble Purposes: The Autobiography of Richard Porter – Surgeon and Evangelist* (Ilkeston: Moorley's, 2nd edn., 2006), pp. 19–20.
[4] Samuel Chadwick, op. cit., p. 17.

5 Johannes Hartl, op. cit., p. 191.
6 See Matthew 18:2–4 and also Mark 14:36 where Jesus calls God 'Abba' – the personal name a son or daughter would call their father in Aramaic.

F is for Fasting

1 See Matthew Porter, *A–Z of Discipleship,* op. cit., p. 24. As well as fasting from food, there are other things we can abstain from, but this is not really what the Bible calls *fasting.* They don't create the same kind of hunger pangs as fasting from food. Nevertheless there are benefits in abstaining from certain things for a while, with the Bible mentioning two things in particular: 1) sex in marriage (see 1 Corinthians 7:5) and 2) alcohol (see Leviticus 10:9). These are usually for a season, although for some God calls them to abstain permanently from such things. In contemporary culture we might add television, social media or the internet. This is not because these things are wrong, but because it's helpful to ensure they don't master us, and to sometimes use the time we would spend on these things for prayer.
2 See Matthew 6:16–18.
3 Although the cumulative effect of so many so-called coincidences in my life combined with the experience of others and the truth of Scripture convinces me that God answers prayer.
4 http://fastingforgod.org/page/6/ (accessed 12.11.18).
5 While this chapter focuses more on the second, all three are important. Note that the 'flesh' is a New Testament term used by the apostle Paul to describe our untamed desires, while the 'spirit' is that part of us that desires God and seeks communion with him. For more from Comer and Bridgetown Church's resources on spiritual disciplines and fasting, see https://practicingtheway .org/practices/fasting (accessed 28.11.18).
6 See Psalm 35:13.
7 This is the main emphasis of Scot McKnight's helpful book *Fasting* (Nashville, TN: Thomas Nelson, 2009).

[8] See Ezra 8:21.

[9] See Daniel 9:3–5; Joel 2:15.

[10] See Judges 20:26.

[11] See 2 Chronicles 20:3.

[12] See Exodus 34:28.

[13] See Psalm 35:13; 2 Samuel 12:16.

[14] Acts 13:2–3.

[15] See Mark 9:29.

[16] See Jonah 3:6–10.

[17] See Daniel 10:2–6.

[18] See Joel 2:12.

[19] Bill Johnson with Jennifer A. Miskov, *Defining Moments* (New Kensington, PA: Whitaker House, 2016), p. 264.

[20] As you begin to fast and show your body that it does not master you, so you will find that you have the ability to be more disciplined in other areas of life too. That's why fasting is often seen as a gateway to all sorts of disciplines, helping form character in us. Mark Batterson says that fasting 'is the discipline that begets discipline. If you can say no to food, you can say no to anything'. Mark Batterson, *If* (Grand Rapids, MI: Baker Books, 2015), p. 49.

[21] See Mark 9:29.

[22] See Matthew 6:16.

[23] ibid.

[24] Taken from *The Circle Maker – Student Edition* by Mark Batterson & Parker Batterson. Copyright © 2012 by Mark Batterson & Parker Batterson. Use by permission of Zondervan. www.zondervan.com.

G is for Gratitude

[1] 'Almighty God, Father of all mercies, we thine unworthy servants do give thee most humble and hearty thanks for all thy goodness and loving-kindness to us and to all men; [particularly to those who desire now to offer up their praises and

Notes

thanksgivings for thy late mercies vouchsafed unto them.] We bless thee for our creation, preservation, and all the blessings of this life; but above all for thine inestimable love in the redemption of the world by our Lord Jesus Christ, for the means of grace, and for the hope of glory. And we beseech thee, give us that due sense of all thy mercies, that our hearts may be unfeignedly thankful, and that we shew forth thy praise, not only with our lips, but in our lives; by giving up ourselves to thy service, and by walking before thee in holiness and righteousness all our days; through Jesus Christ our Lord, to whom with thee and the Holy Ghost be all honour and glory, world without end. Amen.' *The Book of Common Prayer* (London: Church House Publishing, 2004).

2   This story is about gratitude. But it is also a subversive story – about practical love and reconciliation with enemies (as Samaritans were despised by Jews) and how healing and thanksgiving can play a central role in God's unifying kingdom.

3   See 1 Thessalonians 5:18.

4   See, for example, Psalm 118.

5   Ann Voskamp, *One Thousand Gifts* (Grand Rapids, MI: Zondervan, 2010), p. 72.

6   Philippians 4:6, TPT.

H is for Honesty

1   Robert Murray M'Cheyne, cited in editorial of *Themelios*, vol. 23.1 (Leicester: UCCF), October 1996, p. 1.

2   Psalm 5:3.

3   John 4:24.

4   See Ephesians 4:15.

5   See Psalm 139:17.

6   Jim Manney, *A Simple Life-Changing Prayer: Discovering the Power of St Ignatius Loyola's Examen* (Chicago, IL: Loyola Press, 2011), p. 18.

7   2 Kings 19:15a.

212

8   2 Kings 19:15b.
9   2 Kings 19:16.
10 2 Kings 19:17.
11 2 Kings 19:19.

I is for Intercession

1   See Hebrews 7:27.
2   See Hebrews 4:14.
3   Banning Liebscher, *Jesus Culture* (Shippensburg, PA: Destiny Image, 2009), p. 157.
4   See 1 Timothy 2:1–2, TPT.
5   The Monastic Tradition emphasizes contemplative and intercessor prayer and caring for the poor. Often based around community houses (sometimes called monasteries or convents), members would take vows and live simple lives, centred around a rhythm of regular daily prayer and worship.
6   Houses of Prayer are prayer centres where people gather for prayer. While the 'house' is often based in a room or building, it is normally a *community* – a people committed to worship and intercession. See, for example, Beacon House of Prayer in Stoke-on-Trent: http://www.beaconhop.org (accessed 9.11.18).
7   24/7 Prayer describes itself as 'an international, interdenominational movement of prayer, mission and justice; a non-stop prayer meeting that has continued for every minute of this century so far, in over half the countries on Earth', (https://www.24-7prayer.com/about (accessed 9.11.18).
8   See Luke 2:37.
9   Luke 2:38.
10 See 1 John 5:14.
11 Beni Johnson, op. cit., pp. 96–7.
12 John 5:19.
13 See Genesis 18:16–33.
14 Samuel Chadwick, op. cit., p. 18.

J is for Joyful

1. Philippians 1:4, emphasis mine.
2. Psalm 16:11 says that '[God] will fill me with joy in [his] presence'.
3. See John 15:11.
4. This is why Jesus could say to his first disciples, who were about to see him crucified, 'your grief will turn to joy' (John 16:20).
5. See Galatians 5:16.
6. See John 16:22.
7. It is noteworthy that Paul's letter to the Philippians begins and ends with joy. This is how followers of Jesus are called to pray and live.
8. Philippians 4:12.
9. See John 16:24.
10. Ann Voskamp, op. cit., p. 58.
11. See Exodus 15:20.
12. Habakkuk 3:17–18.
13. See Nehemiah 8:10.

K is for Kenosis

1. Theologians call this *the incarnation.*
2. See, for example, Isaiah 53.
3. Philippians 2:6–8, TPT.
4. See Matthew 5:5.
5. Rolland and Heidi Baker, *Reckless Love* (Maidstone: River Publishing, 2014), Day 160.
6. Mark Batterson, *If,* op. cit., p. 55.
7. It probably also explains why the angel calls Mary 'highly favoured' and says, 'The Lord is with you' (Luke 1:28).
8. See Luke 1:38.
9. José Luis González-Balado, *Mother Teresa: in my own words* (Kindle edn. Liguori, MO: Liguori Publications, 1996), ch. 'Generosity'.

¹⁰ This is not to say that prayer lists are wrong or unhelpful. In fact, I use them quite often! My point is that kenosis is about serving *God's* agenda rather than mine, which often means seeking him first and then praying what's on *his* prayer list.

¹¹ See Matthew 6:33.

¹² See 1 Corinthians 13:13.

L is for Liturgy

¹ See 1 Chronicles 15:16–22.

² 'Saint' is a Bible word for anyone who is a follower of Jesus. Many churches have taken the word and also applied it to disciples who are especially holy and have lived a life of devotion to God.

³ That is, it is correct and adheres to the teaching of the Bible.

⁴ Advent is the season approaching Christmas when the church remembers the coming of Christ.

⁵ Lent is the forty-day season approaching Easter when the church encourages self-examination and repentance in preparation for the death and resurrection of Jesus.

⁶ Matthew 15:8.

M is for Morning

¹ See Genesis 22:3–19.

² See Genesis 28:18–19.

³ See Exodus 24:4.

⁴ See Joshua 6:12–27.

⁵ See 1 Samuel 1:19.

⁶ See e.g. Psalm 59:16.

⁷ See Psalm 88:13.

⁸ See Job 1:5.

⁹ See Daniel 6:10–11. The three times were probably in the morning, at noon and in the evening.

Notes

[10] See Luke 2:37.

[11] Mark 1:35.

[12] Mary Kissell: *Before the Days Draw In* (Watford: Instant Apostle, 2018), p. 1.

[13] Cited in Harold Myra, *The One-Year Book of Encouragement: 365 Days of Inspirations and Wisdom for your Spiritual Journey* (Carol Stream, IL: Tyndale House, 2010), p. 305.

[14] Cited in https://lutheranreformation.org/theology/luthers-morning-prayer-model-christians-daily-life (accessed 9.11.18).

[15] Beni Johnson, *The Happy Intercessor*, op. cit., p. 68.

[16] Psalm 5:3.

[17] Anna Koska, cited in Allan Jenkins, *Morning* (London: 4th Estate, 2018), p. 79.

[18] Jamie Oliver, cited in Allan Jenkins, *Morning,* op. cit., p. 22.

[19] Alex Soojung-Kim Pang, *Rest* (London: Penguin, 2017), p. 15.

[20] See 1 Thessalonians 5:17.

[21] Luke 5:16: 'Jesus often withdrew to lonely places and prayed.'

[22] Psalm 55:17.

[23] See Romans 12:12.

[24] Psalm 145:2.

[25] Taken from *The Circle Maker – Student Edition* by Mark Batterson & Parker Batterson. Copyright © 2012 by Mark Batterson & Parker Batterson. Used by permission of Zondervan. www.zondervan.com.

N is for Night

[1] This is probably what the writer of Psalm 119 had in mind when he wrote: 'In the night, LORD, I remember your name' (Psalm 119:55). Jesus prayed in the night, sometimes praying all night – see Luke 6:12.

[2] 'Emerging from this research is an unequivocal message: sleep is the single most effective thing we can do to reset our brain and body health every day.' Matthew Walker, *Why We Sleep* (London: Allen Lane, 2017), p. 8.

3 See Genesis 15:12–13.
4 See Genesis 46:2.
5 See Job 4:13–16.
6 See Matthew 2:19.
7 See Matthew 2:12.
8 See Matthew 27:19.
9 See Acts 2:17–21.
10 Genesis 28:10-22; 31:1–21; 32:9–32; 46:1–7.
11 See 1 Samuel 3:2–15.
12 See 2 Samuel 7:4.
13 See Daniel 2:19.
14 See Zechariah 1:8.
15 See Acts 9:1–18 where God continued to speak to him over three days and three nights in his darkness.
16 Colin Whittaker, *Seven Great Prayer Warriors* (Basingstoke: Marshall Pickering, 1987), p. 150.
17 Ed. William Porter, *For Noble Purposes,* op. cit., p. 76.
18 Song of Songs 5:2.
19 Bill Johnson, in Bill and Beni Johnson et al, *Spiritual Java* (Shippensburg, PA: Destiny Image, 2010), p. 193.
20 See Psalm 63:6–7. In the first instance this probably refers to David being stressed, staying awake and focusing on God. However it may also refer to 'remembering' God deep within as he sleeps.
21 See Psalm 16:7.

O is for Opportunity

1 Colossians 4:2–3.
2 See Acts 12:1–10 and then 11–17.
3 A Gentile is anyone who is not Jewish.
4 See 1 Corinthians 16:8–9.
5 Matthew Porter, *A–Z of Discipleship*, op. cit., p. 74.

Notes

[6] Pete Greig, *Dirty Glory* (Carol Stream, IL: NavPress 2016; London: Hodder & Stoughton, 2018), p. 4.

[7] See e.g. Matthew 7:7–8.

P is for Prophetic

[1] See John 1:1ff.

[2] See John 10:11.

[3] See John 10:27.

[4] This was the case from the beginning of time, with the first humans walking with God and hearing his voice – see Genesis 3:8. When we come to Christ and are born anew, the barriers to knowing God's love and hearing his voice are removed – see Hebrews 4:12–16.

[5] Tania Harris, *God Conversations* (Milton Keynes: Authentic, 2017), p. 213.

[6] See John 6:44.

[7] Saul later changed his name to Paul – the apostle who wrote many of the New Testament letters.

[8] See Acts 9:5.

[9] See Acts 9:17ff.

[10] See Acts 9:10.

[11] Acts 9:10.

[12] For example, through creation, people and circumstances; through art, music and creativity and much more. He made us and the world we inhabit and so has multiple ways to communicate. But he speaks most clearly through his Son, Jesus Christ (see Hebrews 1:1–4) and through the Bible (see 2 Timothy 3:16–17).

[13] Mark Batterson, *Chase the Lion* (New York: Multnomah, 2016), joint edition with *In a Pit with a Lion on a Snowy Day,* p. 324.

[14] For more on this, on how we read the Old Testament through New Testament spectacles, and on how to interpret the Bible, see 'B is for Bible' in my *A–Z of Discipleship* (op. cit).

[15] See Romans 12:1–2.

[16] See 1 Corinthians 14:3.

[17] 1 Corinthians 14:1.

[18] See e.g. Psalm 67; 115; 128 and 129.

[19] For more on the House of Prayer at Ffald-y-Brenin, see Roy Godwin and Dave Roberts, *The Grace Outpouring* (Eastbourne: David C. Cook, 2008). Also: Roy Godwin, *The Way of Blessing* (Colorado Springs, CO: David C. Cook, 2016).

[20] See 1 Thessalonians 5:19–21.

[21] Acts 13:2–3.

Q is for Quiet

[1] See 1 Samuel 1:13.

[2] See e.g. Thomas Keating, *Intimacy with God: An Introduction to Centering Prayer* (New York: Crossroad Publishing Company, 2009).

[3] Psalm 46:7,11.

[4] Psalm 46:10.

[5] Ignatius of Loyola, cited in David Watson, *I Believe in the Church* (London: Hodder & Stoughton, 1978), p. 213.

[6] Wayne Oates, *Nurturing Silence in a Noisy Heart* – cited in Richard Foster, *Freedom of Simplicity* (London: Hodder & Stoughton, 1981, 2005), p. 104.

[7] Samuel Chadwick, op. cit., pp. 25–6.

[8] See e.g. Micah 7:7.

[9] See Lamentations 3:25–26.

[10] See John 13:23; 19:26.

[11] See Revelation 8:1.

[12] See e.g. Erling Kagge's *Silence* (London: Random House, 2017) and Alain Corbin, tr. Jean Birrell, *A History of Silence* (London: Polity Press, 2018).

[13] Blaise Pascal, *Pensées* (trans. A.J. Krailsheimer; London: Penguin, 1995), p. 37.

R is for Relentless

[1] See Matthew 6:7.
[2] See Colossians 4:12.
[3] John Eldredge, *Moving Mountains* (Nashville, TN: Thomas Nelson, 2016), p. 81.
[4] Luke 18:1.
[5] Luke 11:1–13.
[6] See Luke 11:8.
[7] See Luke 11:9–10.
[8] Bill Johnson with Jennifer A. Miskov, *Defining Moments*, op. cit., p. 184.
[9] James 5:14 says: 'Is anyone among you ill? Let them call the elders of the church to pray over them and anoint them with oil in the name of the Lord.'
[10] See Matthew 6:6.
[11] Eugene Peterson, Introduction to 'James', *The Message* Bible.
[12] See e.g. Jeremiah 19:14 – 20:6 and chapters 26 and 28.
[13] See Galatians 5:22–23.
[14] 'Persistence isn't very glamorous. If genius is one percent inspiration and ninety-nine percent perspiration, then as a culture we tend to lionize the one percent. We love its flash and dazzle. But great power lies in the other ninety-nine percent.

   "It's not that I'm so smart," said Einstein . . . "It's that I stay with problems longer."' Susan Caine, *Quiet* (New York: Crown Publishing, 2012), p. 169.

   See also Angela Duckworth's *Grit*, who found through her research that 'It was [the] combination of passion and perseverance that made high achievers special. In a word, they had grit', *Grit* (London: Vermillion, 2016), p. 8.
[15] Pete Greig, op. cit., p. 120.

S is for Sad

[1] Pete Greig, ibid., p. 265.

2 See Job 1:21, KJV.
3 See Psalm 142:6.
4 See John 16:33.
5 See Psalm 42:5,11; 43:5.
6 Johannes Hartl, op. cit., p. 109.
7 See Pete Greig, op. cit., pp. 264–5.
8 David Watson, *Fear No Evil* (London: Hodder & Stoughton, 1984), p. 171.

T is for Tongues

1 A number of lists of God-given gifts are listed in the Bible (see e.g. Romans 12:6–8; 1 Peter 4:11) which are probably meant as examples of gifts rather than exhaustive lists. Tongues is listed in the 1 Corinthian 12 list, which names some of the supernatural gifts that the Holy Spirit gives and loves to distribute especially in the context of prayer and worship.
2 See Acts 10:44–48.
3 See Acts 19:6.
4 These examples and others are listed in John L. Sherrill, *They Speak in Other Tongues* (London: Hodder & Stoughton, 1964), pp. 82–4.
5 See 1 Corinthians 14:16.
6 'For anyone who speaks in a tongue does not speak to people but to God' (1 Corinthians 14:2).
7 See Acts 2:11.
8 See 1 Corinthians 14:14–15.
9 'When we speak in tongues, we are using our voices to give utterance to the expression of our spirits as they commune with the Holy Spirit.' Bill Johnson, *Strengthen Yourself in the Lord* (Shippensburg, PA: Destiny Image, 2007, p. 84).
10 See 1 Corinthians 14:4–20.
11 See 1 Corinthians 14:4.
12 See 1 Corinthians 14:13.
13 See 1 Corinthians 12:10.

Notes

[14] See 1 Corinthians 13:1.

[15] The fact that the Lord would give someone the supernatural ability to speak in an unlearned human language not only shows that God knows and hears the many cultural languages of humanity, but also that he values them.

[16] See Acts 2:8.

[17] See 1 Corinthians 12:30.

[18] See Acts 2:38–41; 8:4–8; 8:9–17; 9:32–42; 13:48–52; 16:11–15; 16:31–34.

[19] See 1 Corinthians 14:18.

[20] See 1 Corinthians 14:5.

[21] See e.g. Matthew 18:3.

[22] See Luke 11:13.

[23] See e.g. Psalm 2:8; Proverbs 25:2; Matthew 18:19; John 14:13.

[24] 'Laying on hands' is mentioned quite a number of times in the Bible. It involves a hand being gently laid on someone in prayer – usually on the shoulder or head. It is often used when commissioning prayers are prayed, both at baptism when someone starts following Jesus (see Acts 19:5–6), and when someone is sent out into a new role (see Acts 6:6). It is especially used in healing prayer (see Mark 6:5), when praying for an infilling of the Holy Spirit (see Acts 8:17) and when blessing people (see Mark 10:16).

[25] See 1 Corinthians 14:1.

[26] Paul says this in 1 Corinthians 14:12.

[27] Bill Johnson, *Strengthen Yourself in the Lord* (Shippensburg, PA: Destiny Image, 2007), p. 88.

[28] Guy Chevreau, *Pray with Fire* (London: Marshall Pickering, 1995), p. 97.

U is for Unanswered

[1] Eugene Peterson helpfully explains it like this: 'To the objection "I prayed and cried out for help, but no help came," the answer is

"But it did. . . . You were looking for something quite different, perhaps, but God brought the help that would change your life into health, into wholeness for eternity . . ." Instead of asking why the help has not come, the person at prayer learns to look carefully at what is actually going on in his life or her life, . . . and ask, "Could this be the help he is providing? I never thought of *this* in terms of help, but maybe it is."' Eugene H. Peterson, *God's Message for Each Day* (Nashville, TN: Thomas Nelson, 2006), p. 297.

[2] See Psalm 17:6.

[3] See Psalm 13:1,3.

[4] See 1 John 5:14.

[5] See Jeremiah 29:11.

[6] PRAYER – LETTERS TO MALCOLM by CS Lewis © CS Lewis Pte Ltd 1963, 1964.

[7] See Ecclesiastes 3:1,11; Psalm 31:15.

[8] See James 4:3.

[9] See Psalm 66:18; Proverbs 21:13.

[10] Mark 11:24–26.

[11] See Ephesians 6:12–20.

[12] See Romans 8:28.

[13] See 1 Corinthians 13:12.

[14] Philip Yancey's helpful book, *Prayer,* devotes two chapters to unanswered prayer, and concludes, 'No human being, no matter how wise or how spiritual, can interpret the ways of God, explain why one miracle and not another, why an apparent intervention here and not there. Along with the apostle Paul, we can only wait, and trust.' Philip Yancey, *Prayer* (Grand Rapids, MI: Zondervan, 2006), p. 247.

[15] See 2 Corinthians 12:7–9.

[16] See Pete Greig, *God on Mute: Engaging the Silence of Unanswered Prayer* (Eastbourne: Kingsway, 2007), p. 19.

[17] Mark Batterson & Parker Batterson, *The Circle Maker – Student Edition*, op. cit, p. 110.

V is for Vision

[1] Visionary prayer includes praying for nations. Moses prayed such prayers, for example saying to God in thanksgiving: 'What other nation is so great as to have their gods there near them the way the LORD our God is near us whenever we pray to him?' (Deuteronomy 4:7).

[2] See Ephesians 3:20.

[3] See Genesis 15:5.

[4] See Romans 4:11.

[5] See Esther 4:14.

[6] See Nehemiah 1:4–11.

[7] See Luke 2:36–38.

[8] See ijmuk.org (accessed 22.11.18).

[9] Wesley Duewel, *Mighty Prevailing Prayer* (Grand Rapids, MI: Zondervan, 1990), p. 27.

[10] Kris Vallotton, *The Supernatural Ways of Royalty* (Shippensburg, PA: Destiny Image, 2006), p. 215.

[11] Samuel Chadwick, op. cit., p. 80.

W is for Warfare

[1] C.S. Lewis, *Christian Reflections* (Grand Rapids, MI: Eerdmans, 1967), p. 33.

[2] Widely and reputably attributed to Samuel Chadwick, but source unknown. Cited, for example, in Tom Cannon, *We Speak to Nations* (Gray, TN: Preacher's Kid Press, 2006), p. 151.

[3] Satan is not equal in power of authority with God. He is a fallen angel who, although influential, is equivalent to the archangel Michael. He was mortally wounded by Christ at the cross, and his fate is sealed.

[4] See e.g. Psalm 35:1: 'Contend . . . with those who contend with me; fight against those who fight against me.'

[5] See Acts 4:1–31.

[6] Daniel 9:19.

[7] See e.g. Matthew 5:43–48.

8   See e.g. 2 Chronicles 20:21 where 'Jehoshaphat appointed men to sing to the LORD and to praise him for the splendour of his holiness as they went out at the head of the army . . . '

9   See Psalm 144:1.

10 See James 4:6–10.

11 See Luke 6:27; 10:25–37.

12 See Galatians 5:16 (NKJV).

13 See: https://www.amazon.co.uk/Limitless-Gods-Creative-Mandate-Church/dp/1539874931 (accessed 19.11.18).

X is for eXamen

1   Ignatius (1491–1556) lived in Spain and founded a significant prayerful missionary movement.

2   Ignatius actually taught that the Examen should be used at noon as well as the end of the day, although many these days use it as a bedtime tool for prayer.

3   See Jim Massey, op. cit., where he says that the Latin root also includes a sense of 'weighing or judging something'.

4   There are variations to the five-step model. What I suggest is mainly based on the steps advocated by Jim Massey, op. cit., with elements also taken from: https://www.ignatianspirituality.com/ignatian-prayer/the-examen/how-can-i-pray (accessed 9.11.18).

5   Proverbs 4:23–26.

6   Ecclesiastes 5:2.

7   See Psalm 141:2.

8   Eugene H. Peterson, *Christ Plays in Ten Thousand Places* (London: Hodder & Stoughton, 2005), p. 274.

Y is for Yearning

1   See Romans 8:26, NIV and TPT.

2   See Pete Greig, op. cit., p. 130.

Notes

[3] Isaiah 26:8–9.

[4] Psalm 63:1.

[5] Praying people are described as being like 'watchmen' on a number of occasions in the Bible. See e.g. Psalm 130:6. The metaphor is used most explicitly in Isaiah 62:6: 'I have posted watchmen on your walls, Jerusalem; they will never be silent day or night. You who call on the LORD, give yourself no rest, and give him no rest till he establishes Jerusalem and makes her the praise of the earth.'

[6] See Psalm 42:1–16.

[7] See 1 Timothy 2:4.

[8] Cited in Andrew A. Bonar, *Memoirs & Remains of Robert Murray M'Cheyne* (Boston, MA: Wentworth Press, 1844, 2016), p. 366.

Z is for Zero

[1] Matthew Porter, op. cit., p. 47.

[2] See e.g. Acts 17:27 which describes God wanting people to 'reach out for him and find him' for 'he is not far from any one of us'.

[3] Wesley Duewel, op. cit., p. 32.

[4] See Genesis 3:9–12.

[5] 'The sin of prayerlessness is a proof for the ordinary Christian or minister that the life of God is in deadly sickness and weakness.' Andrew Murray, *The Prayer Life* (Seaside, OR: Rough Draft Printing, 1912, 2013), p. 8.

[6] James 4:2.

[7] See Isaiah 43:22–28.

[8] Which is why Jesus tells us to pray 'lead us not into temptation' (see Matthew 6:13).

[9] See Matthew 4:1ff.

[10] Matthew 26:41.

[11] Wesley Duewel, op. cit., p. 30.

[12] This is a phrase used by the writer of Judges to describe the ethical laxity of those who live with no reference to God. See e.g. Judges 17:6 and 21:25.

[13] See Zephaniah 3:2.

[14] See Zephaniah 3:5.

[15] John 15:6.

[16] See Revelation 3:20.

[17] Samuel Chadwick, op. cit., p. 23.

[18] Jim Cymbala, *Fresh Wind, Fresh Fire* (Grand Rapids, MI: Zondervan, 1997), p. 19.

[19] 2 Chronicles 7:14.

[20] In days before gender-neutral language was important.

[21] Samuel Chadwick, ibid., p. 11.

Index

Abraham, patriarch 68–9, 93, 101, 166
Ambrose of Milan 6
Amen 37, 91, 110
Anna, prophetess 67, 93, 166
Anselm, St 6
Anson, Liz 105
Anthony, St 94
armour of God 159, 174–9
Asaph, psalm writer 87–8
Augustine, St 94

Baker, Heidi & Rolland 11, 81, 85
Barnett, Barney (Austin) 43–4
Barton, Ruth Haley 131
Basil, St 44
Bath, Hannah 127
Batterson, Mark 47, 82, 98, 161, 172, 211
Belfrey, The, York 13, 16, 53, 66, 111, 127, 145, 187, 191, 207
Benedict, St 94
Bible, The 1, 37, 71, 87, 93, 119, 120, 200, 209, 218
Blackwell, David 139

Chadwick, Samuel 39, 42, 70, 127, 170, 173, 189–90, 199, 201, 206

Chambers, Oswald 29, 33
Chevreau, Guy 154
Cho, Paul Y. 15
Clapham Sect 94
Clement of Alexandria 1
Common Worship 26, 99, 107
Cymbala, Jim 200, 202

Daniel, prophet 69, 93, 102, 176, 179, 215
David, king of Israel 25, 29, 58, 60, 88, 93, 96, 97, 105, 157, 177, 184, 188
Dearden, Richard 187
Dearden, Sophie 37
Deuwel, Wesley 168, 193, 198
devil, the 24, 173–4, 188, 224

Eldredge, John 134
Elkanah 93
Engle, Lou 68
Esther 166

Ffald-y-Brenin, House of Prayer 121
Fletcher, James 30

General Thanksgiving, the 51, 89
grace 54–5, 160, 212

Greig, Pete 19, 29, 138, 139, 141, 161, 163
Guyon, Madam 102

Habakkuk, prophet 76–7
Hannah, mother of Samuel 125
Harris, Tania 117
Hartl, Johannes 31, 40, 78, 144
Harvey, E.F. & L. 115
Hezekiah, king of Israel 60–61
Huggett, Joyce 123

Ignatius of Loyola, St 126, 181–2, 225
imagination 17, 167, 170, 184, 185
Isaiah, prophet 46, 60, 188, 191, 226

Jacob, patriarch 69, 93, 101, 102
James, brother of John 110
James, writer of Letter of James 137
Jeremiah, prophet 137, 220
Jesus – death and resurrection 7, 65, 79, 144, 177, 215
  – model for prayer 13, 51, 71, 79
  – teaching on prayer 5, 13, 22, 43, 45, 113, 133
Job 60, 93, 102, 137, 142–3
Johnson, Beni 7, 68, 72, 95
Johnson, Bill 6, 45, 104, 105, 135, 153
Joseph 102
journalling 17, 61, 122, 169

Keating, Thomas 219
Kilravock Castle 109–10
Kingdom of God 5, 14, 38, 45, 47, 65, 74, 80, 145, 169–70, 177, 205, 212
Korah, sons of 93

Koska, Anna 96
lament 141–2, 145
Lewis, C.S. 158, 173
Liebscher, Banning 66
Lord's Prayer, The 5, 7, 38, 45, 87, 90, 91, 183, 203
Ludlam, Margaret 61

Manney, Jim 59, 186
Mathews, R. Arthur 179
M'Cheyne, Robert Murray 57, 226
miracles 55, 136, 223
Moody, D.L. 136
Moses, prophet 36–7, 69, 93, 224
Müller, George 94
Myers, Paul 112

Nathan, prophet 102
Nee, Watchman 94
Northumbria Community 92

Oloyede, Jonathan 176

Pascal, Blaise 129
Paul, apostle 55, 58, 66, 73, 74, 79, 102, 109, 111, 119, 133, 150, 152, 160, 165, 167, 176, 187, 210, 214, 218, 222, 223
persecuted church 67
Peterson, Eugene 137, 185, 205, 222
Pilate's wife 102
Porter, Christine 22, 141–2
Porter, Karen 80, 135
Porter, Matthew 15, 210
Porter, Richard 103
Porter, Sam 27, 73, 94, 136, 150, 158
Porter, William 81, 135, 141
prayer – audacious 134
  – authority, praying with 13, 168

Index

prayer (*Continued*)
- Bible, praying with 1, 68, 83, 87, 119, 206
- blessing 90, 120–21
- centring 125
- contemplative 126, 128, 213
- definition of 1
- faith, praying with 13–18, 55, 61, 169–70
- hands, laying on 122, 153, 207, 222
- healing 14, 82, 105, 120, 136, 189, 222
- meetings & praying with others 54, 61, 66–7, 74, 122, 167, 190, 213
- obedient 18, 82, 202
- oil, anointing with 136, 220
- please 1, 8, 21, 38, 203
- praise 9, 16, 52, 57, 88, 97, 141, 149–50, 168, 177, 211
- prayer ministry 207
- silent 29, 125–9
- sorry 9, 21–5, 38, 120, 183, 203
- Spirit, Holy, being filled with 62, 82, 188, 222
- supplication 24, 65, 183, 199
- thank you 21, 35, 38, 51–5, 95, 203
- worship 5–9, 15, 30, 66, 88, 104–5, 119, 122, 177, 182, 200
prayerfulness 16, 77, 83, 88, 118, 137, 155, 181, 185, 190, 199
Pullinger, Jackie 154, 156

St Cuthbert's House of Prayer, York 8, 28, 30, 37, 66

St Michael le Belfrey, York, *see* Belfrey, The, York
Samuel, prophet 102
Satan, *see* devil, the
Saul, *see* Paul
Sentamu, John, Archbishop of York 88
Simeon, Charles 94
Simpson, Roger 53
Smith, Barry 18
Smith, Jim 103
Solomon, king of Israel 8, 104, 183
Stephenson, Barrie 165
Stott, John 94
Swaffield-Bray, Esther 167

Teresa of Avila 94
Teresa of Calcutta, Mother 83, 165
testimony 16, 75, 81, 173

Voskamp, Ann 55, 56, 76

Wade, Francis 6
Wallis, Arthur 49
Watson, David 111, 145, 148, 219
Welby, Justin, Archbishop of Canterbury 113
Welch, John 190
Wesley, John 94
Wimber, John 82
Winks, Steve 57–8
wise men, the 102

Yancey, Philip 223
Young, William P. 63

Zechariah, prophet 102